SAUSAGE

A COUNTRY-BY-COUNTRY PHOTOGRAPHIC GUIDE WITH RECIPES

SAUSAGE

A COUNTRY-BY-COUNTRY PHOTOGRAPHIC GUIDE WITH RECIPES

Nichola Fletcher

Recipes by Caroline Bretherton

LONDON, NEW YORK, MELBOURNE,
MUNICH, AND DELHI

US Editors Rachel Bozek and Rebecca Warren
Copy Editor Lucy Bannell
Photographers Peter Anderson, William Reavell,
Angela Coppola, Julie Renouf, Tim de Neefe,
Stuart West, William Shaw, and Deepak Aggarwal

DK UK
Editor Shashwati Tia Sarkar
Project Art Editor Kathryn Wilding
Editorial Assistants David Fentiman
and Charlotte Morgan-Nwokenna
Managing Editor Dawn Henderson
Managing Art Editor Christine Keilty
Senior Jacket Creative Nicola Powling
Senior Production Editor Clare McLean
Production Controller Claire Pearson
Creative Technical Support Sonia Charbonnier

DK INDIA
Project Editor Charis Bhagianathan
Senior Art Editor Balwant Singh
Art Editor Mahua Sharma
Assistant Editor Priyanka Chatterjee
Assistant Art Editor Rohit Walia
Managing Editor Glenda Fernandes
Managing Art Editor Navidita Thapa
CTS Manager Sunil Sharma
DTP Operator Satish Chandra Gaur

First American Edition, 2012

Published in the United States by
DK Publishing
375 Hudson Street
New York, New York 10014

12 13 14   10 9 8 7 6 5 4 3 2 1

001—181874—Apr/2012

Published in Great Britain by Dorling Kindersley Limited.

A catalog record for this book is available from
the Library of Congress.

ISBN 978-0-7566-8983-4

DK books are available at special discounts when purchased in
bulk for sales promotions, premiums, fund-raising, or educational
use. For details, contact: DK Publishing Special Markets, 375 Hudson
Street, New York, New York 10014 or SpecialSales@dk.com.

Color reproduction by Colourscan, Singapore

Printed and bound in China by Leo

Discover more at www.dk.com

Contents

Foreword

Whenever I mentioned to someone that I was writing a book about sausages, they would invariably smile with delight and enthusiastically tell me about their favorite type, or a fond memory. For everyone loves sausages; even the most sophisticated gourmet finds them irresistible.

Part of the reason for this fondness is that sausages are part of our childhood and they spark the best sort of memories: of barbecues on the beach, or campfires in the woods; going to a football game with dad, or enjoying a cozy Sunday breakfast. They also evoke strong feelings of national pride. British people adore their bready bangers. Germans, on the other hand, are proud of their sausages' high meat content and their sausage laws dating back hundreds of years. I recently met an Italian blacksmith living in France who carries an electric meat slicer in the trunk of his car because, coming from Bologna, he is convinced that no Frenchman will be capable of slicing his *salame* as paper-thin as it should be.

The more I delved into this world of sausages, the more delightful examples I discovered. As well as beautiful ruby-red salami and nut-brown kiełbasa, there are comically shaped, bulbous creations stuffed into stomachs, there are long dried sticks, gleaming fresh coils, tiny round sausages, and more. Among those with more unusual ingredients, there are startling sausages made green with spinach, blood sausages pungent with sweet potato leaves, and cuttlefish sausages teamed with fermented rice. We have scoured the world to find excellent examples but some of the more bizarre specimens have not made it to these pages. The flour-filled lamb's lung made by the Uighurs, the strawberry-flavored Mexican chorizo, and the fish sausages from Finland are perhaps fodder for a future book.

I hope you will enjoy discovering all these sausages as much as I did, and savor them by making the hearty recipes in this book. For above all, hot sausages are the best comfort food. Served up with some good mashed potatoes or tangy sauerkraut, or even just on a roll with ketchup, they induce what is known as "hygge." It's a Danish word, meaning a warm, cozy feeling of well-being. Soul food. But it could just as well be translated as "sausage."

All about sausages

Mankind has been making sausages for thousands of years. The original reason for creating them was to make use of every scrap of meat but, millennia later, a world of sausages has evolved to suit different religions, climates, and available ingredients.

What is a sausage?

Not surprisingly, each country has its own idea of what a "proper" sausage should (or should not) be. In the Czech Republic, the idea that salami is a sausage is ludicrous, and to British people, head cheese is a meat preparation and definitely not a sausage. In this book, we have taken the view that if it is encased in a skin then it is a sausage. This gave us the opportunity to accommodate the many international interpretations of the word "sausage."

Bauern-Rotwurst p15
Ingredients added to blood sausages reflect what is available locally. This German one is studded with pork.

As a result, we have included meatless sausages, and even some skinless examples such as mititei (see page 113), which have wriggled into these pages by virtue of their regional importance.

Sausage origins

Where sausages were first made is a fact that has been lost in the mists of time, but we do know that they were being made in the Middle East in the Bronze Age, that they were popular in ancient Greece and Roman Italy, and that the Chinese recorded sausages as far back as the seventh century CE. Over the centuries, the sausage has been adapted to suit both culture and climate, so that there are many different opinions about what ought to be put into a sausage. Some countries make them from cheaper off-cuts of meat, perhaps including skin, ears, or even mechanically recovered meat (MRM), to produce tasty but cheap food. In these countries, the notion of padding out sausages by adding barley, rice, oatmeal, or twice-baked biscuits seems perfectly sensible. Other cultures select more expensive cuts, have strict regulations surrounding their processing, and disapprove of using anything other than pure meat and spices. Throughout the world, gluts of seasonal vegetables, too, have evolved into speciality sausages.

The well-traveled sausage

People are so attached to the sausages of their homeland that it is inevitable that when they travel, they take their recipes with them. In this way, the nations that colonized other countries in the past left a legacy of sausages that were adapted to local conditions, ingredients, and customs. For instance, the salamis, Frankfurters, chorizos, and bologna sausages found in Australia, New Zealand, India, and almost the whole of the Americas have evolved from the sausages of another continent. In many cases, although they retain the same name, the sausage itself is quite different from the original version. Conversely, foreign sausages are rarely found in the countries of origin (Spain, Portugal, Germany, Poland, or Italy). However, since the boundaries of many countries have changed over the centuries, almost identical sausages will be found on either side of the borders where these countries merge.

Our sausages to savor

With many thousands of sausages to choose from, there were some hard decisions to be made about what we could include in the book, so we have made our selections reflect the flavor and texture of each country by including typically characteristic examples and some famous regional varieties. In most countries there are many local variations so do seek them out, armed with the knowledge of the authentic types of that region found in this book. Some sausages are available only in the autumn and winter, so if you have the opportunity, try chouriço with honey in the Portuguese vineyards, or Pormonier sausages in Savoie, which are made with chard.

Goan chorizo p135
Goa was a Portuguese colony, but this punchy sausage has Indian spices as well as the paprika typical of chorizo.

What makes a good sausage?

Three elements go into making a really good sausage. The ingredients play a crucial part, whether it is the meat, the spices and herbs, or the liquids. The type of sausage skin will also define the character of the sausage. Finally, there is the way in which the sausage is made—there is a great difference between an artisan butcher's sausage and one that has been made by the thousand in a factory.

Some of the finest sausages in the world are made from simply pork, salt, and pepper. But the pork must be superb; there is a huge difference in quality between the pork from semi-wild Iberian black pigs and that from industrially produced pigs with controlled diets. Also, good ingredients must be packed into good skins. Although there are many fine sausages made in synthetic casings, the very best are made with natural skins, which expand and contract with the sausage, giving a more perfect fit; this is especially the case with dried sausages. Finally, the care with which the meat is chopped, cured, dried, smoked, or cooked all add to the making of the perfect sausage.

Adding local flavor

Local preferences determine what additional flavorings are used, and some of them define the style of a particular country. For example, paprika (dried red pepper), is typical of both Hungarian sausages and chorizo, and in these countries each region has its own variety of pepper. Garlic, too, is a distinguishing flavor in Polish and South East Asian sausages. In areas where meat was scarce, some unusual ingredients—either seasonally or locally available—were incorporated to make the meat last longer Ingredients such as chestnuts, spinach, currants, and potatoes, and even squid, shrimp, egg yolks, and bones, have produced some of the most unexpectedly delicious sausages in the world.

Salame di Varzi p61
The high quality of the pork and the lengthy drying period give this sausage its white yeasty mold and distinctive flavor.

Choosing and storing sausages

Find artisan sausages at markets, in butchers' shops, and on specialist websites. Check the ingredients, look at the skins, and always follow the manufacturer's directions for storage.

Fresh sausages are made from minced meat mixed with other ingredients, and are therefore "high risk." Even if containing preservatives, they must be kept refrigerated and used within their use-by date.

Cured sausages have a longer shelf-life than fresh sausages but this can vary considerably. Most are best stored in the refrigerator.

Some cured and partially dried sausages are best kept refrigerated, but others will keep almost indefinitely without refrigeration. Check the label to be sure.

Fully dried sausages, whether cured or not, do not need refrigerating but should be kept cool to prevent them becoming greasy. The skins should not be eaten.

BUYING THE REAL DEAL

Since traditional sausages can have many interpretations, throughout the European Union there is a scheme to protect the ingredients and manufacture of original local products. If you see one of the following used on a label, the sausage is guaranteed to be the original authentic version.

PDO (DOP): Protected Designation of Origin

PGI (IGP): Protected Geographical Indication

TSG: Traditional Speciality Guaranteed

AOC: Appellation d'Origine Contrôlée (a scheme used in some French-speaking nations).

Saucisson Vaudois PGI p41
The authentic version is irregular in shape.

Types of sausages

There are many different methods of transforming basic ingredients into sausages. To provide a simple way of recognizing them, this book divides the sausages into five basic types. Many sausages combine two or more of these methods—each one affects the taste and texture of the resulting sausage.

Fresh sausages

Made from uncooked meat that is minced or chopped then mixed with spices, and sometimes binders. The filling is put into natural or collagen casings and occasionally cold smoked. Fresh sausages are always cooked before eating.
TO ENJOY: fry, grill, barbecue, stew, bake, or use in recipes. Ensure they are well cooked all the way through.

Farmhouse sausage p80
Most British sausages are fresh.

Cured sausages

Made from meat mixed with curing salts or wine vinegar and left to ferment, which coagulates the meat and kills bacteria. Curing gives a typical tangy (or sour) flavor. Some are smoked; hot smoking increases the shelf life.
TO ENJOY: eat soft, spreadable types raw. Firmer types can be eaten raw, or gently simmered, or used in stews.

Ossenworste p93
Soft, cured sausages like this one are eaten raw.

Cooked sausages

There are two categories of cooked sausages. The first category comprises those that are made from uncooked raw ingredients, then cooked. It includes mortadella and Frankfurter types, which are made from finely minced meat, often pounded to a paste, that is put into skins and cooked. Frankfurter types are sometimes called "scalded sausages." Blood sausages are also in the first category: fresh or reconstituted blood is mixed with ingredients such as grains, cubes of fat, or meat, filled into skins, and cooked. Some are hot smoked, a few are dried.

The second category are those sausages made from precooked ingredients—cooked meat or offal that is chopped or minced, mixed with flavorings, put into wide skins, and cooked again. They're usually served as cold cuts, and some, like haggis, are reheated to serve.
TO ENJOY: eat mortadella types cold and thinly sliced. Grill, fry, or boil Frankfurter types; ensure they are heated right through. Slice and fry blood sausages, or simmer them whole; some are sliced and eaten cold. Spread liver sausages on bread; slice head cheese and eat cold.

Leverpølse p96
Made from pre-cooked meats, liver sausages are soft.

Kaszanka p101
Blood sausages are popular the world over.

Frankfurter Würstchen p18
Simmer scalded sausages gently rather than boiling too hard.

Cured and dried sausages

These are cured, but then dried. A brief drying period firms the texture and intensifies flavor, but the finished sausage still needs refrigerating. Prolonged drying makes a harder sausage that can be thinly sliced; they keep for longer and don't need refrigeration. Many are smoked before drying.

TO ENJOY: partially dried ones can be cooked in dishes, but most types are eaten raw. Slice hard sausages thinly; cut softer ones a little thicker. Remove synthetic skins.

Dried sausages

Made from chopped or minced meat, fat, and flavorings, which are filled into skins and dried. Drying intensifies the flavors as well as preserving the meat. They are not cured, so they taste more purely of the meat they are made from and are usually harder. Some are hot or cold smoked, too.

TO ENJOY: slice hard dried sausages paper-thin to appreciate the flavor at its best. Eat raw, or use for pizza toppings, or in cooked dishes. Remove the outer skins before eating.

Chorizo Gallego p69
Part-dried cured sausages are good for cooking.

Salame Toscano p63
Dried sausages taste best sliced very thinly.

What this book tells you

A guide to the catalog and symbols.

Flags represent the countries of origin of the sausages displayed on a page.

Names are in the language of the sausage's origin, except for those that do not use the Roman alphabet. Protected geographical status is also mentioned here.

The ingredients, flavors, and defining characteristics of each sausage is described. Salt is used in every sausage so is not mentioned to avoid repetition.

Maps show which country or countries produce the sausage. Specific regions or towns associated with its provenance are plotted with black dots. Where there is no dot, the sausage is made more widely.

Size icons represent the scale relative to other sausages— "extra small," "small," "medium," "large," and "extra large."

MEAT ICONS

Turkey Pheasant Goose Chicken Duck Ostrich

Beef Veal Horse Donkey Lamb

Mutton Goat Venison Springbok Moose\Elk

Reindeer Wild Boar Pork Kangaroo Rabbit

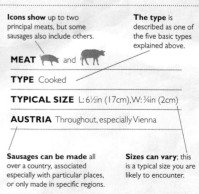

Icons show up to two principal meats, but some sausages also include others.

The type is described as one of the five basic types explained above.

MEAT and

TYPE Cooked

TYPICAL SIZE L: 6½in (17cm), W: ¾in (2cm)

AUSTRIA Throughout, especially Vienna

Sausages can be made all over a country, associated especially with particular places, or only made in specific regions.

Sizes can vary; this is a typical size you are likely to encounter.

Sausages to Savor

THE BEST FROM AROUND THE WORLD

GERMANY

Any country that boasts of 1,000 different sausages must earn the title, "the land of the sausage." Visitors to Germany encounter a magnificent array of local variations, each a different flavor, shape, and size. They have been featured in German festivities since medieval times, when people paraded giant sausages through the streets or wore necklaces of sausages during celebrations, and today they play a huge part in German beer festivals, and as street food.

All Germanic sausages fall into three main categories. The meat for *Rohwurst* is cured by fermentation; it is traditionally cold smoked or air dried and eaten raw. *Brühwurst* is made from raw meat that is pounded and then cooked to 160°F (72°C) so it remains firm; they are eaten either as cold cuts or cooked again (*Bratwurst* is always recooked). *Kochwurst* and *Sülzwurst* are made from precooked meats that are minced, stuffed into casings, and then cooked again to 175°F (80°C). These are mostly eaten cold, either sliced or as spreadable pastes, but some are recooked.

Ahle Wurst

The flavor of this *Rohwurst* comes from its slow maturation and superb pork from specially heavy pigs. The seasoning varies from simple pepper to a mixture of spices. It is sometimes smoked.

MEAT 🐖

TYPE Cured and dried

TYPICAL SIZE L: 10in (25cm), W: 2in (5cm)

GERMANY North Hesse

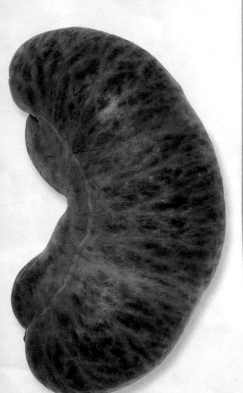

Bauern-Rotwurst

A rustic, "farmhouse" style of *Kochwurst* with chunks of pork meat and fat studding the red-colored blood. It is usually quite spicy and smoked. There are many different shapes, including this one stuffed into caecum (a bulbous intestine).

MEAT

TYPE Cooked

TYPICAL SIZE L: 7in (18cm), W: 3in (8cm)

GERMANY Throughout

Bierschinken

This is a large scalded *Brühwurst* made from very finely ground pork, attractively marbled with large chunks of ham and sometimes pistachio nuts. It is usually eaten cold and thinly sliced.

MEAT

TYPE Cooked

TYPICAL SIZE L: 10in (25cm), W: 4in (10cm)

GERMANY Throughout

Bierwurst

A scalded *Brühwurst* of pork, or pork and beef, evenly speckled with fat, and flavored with black peppercorns, mustard seed, paprika, and garlic (but no beer). It is smoked to a deep brown and often eaten with a glass of beer.

MEAT and

TYPE Cooked

TYPICAL SIZE L: 8in (20cm), W: 4in (10cm)

GERMANY Throughout

15

Bockwurst

A Frankfurter-type of *Brühwurst* traditionally made from veal and pork and lightly smoked, but also made from lamb and poultry. It is spiced with white pepper and paprika, and sometimes speckled with herbs.

MEAT 🐑 and 🐖

TYPE Cooked

TYPICAL SIZE L: 4in (10cm), W: 1in (3cm)

GERMANY Throughout, especially Berlin

Braunschweiger

Hailing from Germany's sausage-making center, this is a soft, spreadable *Rohwurst* made from coarsely minced pork, beef, and back fat, and sometimes garlic or caraway. This is cured and eaten raw.

MEAT 🐖 and 🐄

TYPE Cured and dried

TYPICAL SIZE L: 7in (18cm), W: 1½in (4cm)

GERMANY Throughout, originally Brunswick, Lower Saxony

Bregenwurst

A spreadable *Rohwurst* made from pork and pork belly and, originally, oats and flour. Made into rings and lightly smoked, it can be eaten raw, but is traditionally cooked and served with kale.

MEAT 🐖

TYPE Cured

TYPICAL SIZE L: 10in (25cm), W: 1in (3cm)

GERMANY Lower Saxony

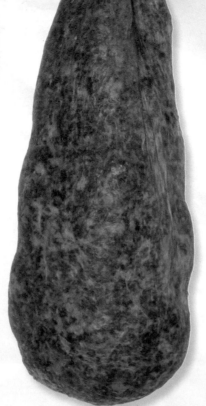

Deutsche Salami

German salami is a hard *Rohwurst* sausage made from pork, beef, and back fat that is usually coarsely minced for a rustic texture. It is flavored with peppercorns and garlic, and is normally smoked.

MEAT and

TYPE Cured and dried

TYPICAL SIZE L: 12in (30cm), W: 4in (10cm)

GERMANY Throughout

Eichsfelder Feldkieker

This chopped-pork *Rohwurst* was originally drop-shaped, as it was sewn into a pig's bladder, then smoked and dried for up to a year. Now it comes in several shapes.

MEAT

TYPE Cured and dried

TYPICAL SIZE L: 8in (20cm), W: 5in (13cm)

GERMANY Eichsfeld, Thuringia

Feste Runde

A slim, speckled pork *Rohwurst* from the Eichfeld region of Thuringia, flavored with black peppercorns and garlic, then cured and dried to a deep brown. *Dürre Runde* is similar, but typically originating from North Hesse.

MEAT

TYPE Cured and dried

TYPICAL SIZE L: 12in (30cm), W: 2in (5cm)

GERMANY Eichsfeld, Thuringia

17

Flönz

Little pieces of pork rind and fat stud this dark red blood sausage, which is smoked for extra flavor. This *Kochwurst* is eaten either cold with mustard, or hot with apples and onions.

MEAT 🐷

TYPE Cooked

TYPICAL SIZE L: 13½in (35cm), W: 1½in (4cm)

GERMANY Cologne, Rhineland

Frankfurter Würstchen

Frankfurt's most famous *Brühwurst* is made from finely ground pork and beef, contained in a slim sheep's casing. It is lightly smoked to a pale to golden brown color, and simmered before eating.

MEAT 🐷 and 🐮

TYPE Cooked

TYPICAL SIZE L: 6in (15cm), W: ¾in (2cm)

GERMANY Frankfurt, Hesse

Gelbwurst

Distinctive for its bright yellow skin, this is a smooth, creamy colored *Brühwurst*. Originally including brain, it is now made from pork and veal flavored with ginger, nutmeg, and lemon. It is eaten cold on bread.

MEAT 🐷 and 🐑

TYPE Cooked

TYPICAL SIZE L: 12in (30cm), W: 2in (5cm)

GERMANY Bavaria

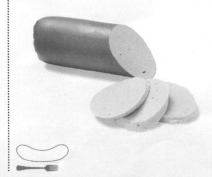

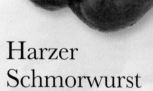

Graupenwurst

A speciality of northeastern Germany, this *Kochwurst* is made from pig's blood and pork rind bound together with barley, and flavored with marjoram. It is eaten with sauerkraut and boiled potatoes.

MEAT 🐖

TYPE Cooked

TYPICAL SIZE L: 6in (15cm), W: 1in (3cm)

GERMANY Mecklenburg West Pomerania

Gutsleberwurst

Mild in flavor, this is a liver *Kochwurst* sausage with chunks of pork, fat, and liver interspersed throughout the smooth paste. Some versions have a rustic, bulbous appearance and are smoked.

MEAT 🐖

TYPE Cooked

TYPICAL SIZE L: 10in (25cm), W: 2¾in (7cm)

GERMANY Throughout, especially Thuringia

Harzer Schmorwurst

This hearty *Rohwurst* is a speciality from the Harz mountains. It is flavored with caraway seed, then lightly smoked. Sometimes it is scalded. It can be eaten cold, or cooked and served with green cabbage.

MEAT 🐖

TYPE Cooked

TYPICAL SIZE L: 7in (18cm), W: 1in (3cm)

GERMANY Harz, Lower Saxony

19

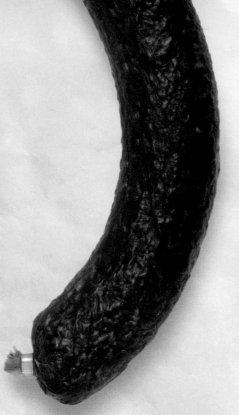

Hirschsalami

Venison makes this deep red *Rohwurst* salami leaner than most. The best are made from pure venison meat, others add up to 60 percent fatty pork to keep the sausage moist. It is usually smoked.

MEAT 🦌

TYPE Cured and dried

TYPICAL SIZE L: 8in (20cm), W: 2½in (6cm)

GERMANY Throughout

Hofer Rindfleischwurst

A *Rohwurst* made from finely minced lean beef, though some also contain some pork and back fat. Well spiced with garlic, cloves, and black pepper, it is briefly dried.

MEAT 🐖

TYPE Cured

TYPICAL SIZE L: 5in (12cm), W: 2in (5cm)

GERMANY Bavaria

Jagdwurst

This is a large hunter's sausage made from finely minced lean pork or turkey, interspersed with small chunks of pork or beef. Sometimes smoked, this Bologna-style *Brühwurst* is thinly sliced and eaten cold.

MEAT 🐖 or 🦃

TYPE Cooked

TYPICAL SIZE L: 12in (30cm), W: 4in (10cm)

GERMANY Throughout

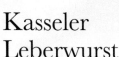

Kalbsleberwurst

Made from calf's liver and pork, this is a high-quality, creamy *Kochwurst* with a higher protein content than most liver sausage. This spreading sausage goes particularly well with dark German pumpernickel.

MEAT and

TYPE Cooked

TYPICAL SIZE L: 10in (25cm), W: 2½in (6cm)

GERMANY Throughout

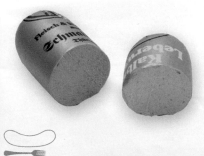

Kartoffelwurst

This wrinkled *Kochwurst* contains very little fat as it uses potato cubes instead of pork fat. The potato is mixed with pork, blood, or other meats, such as beef. Similar is *Grumbeerewurst*, which sometimes includes carrots.

MEAT or

TYPE Cooked

TYPICAL SIZE L: 18in (45cm), W: 1½in (4cm)

GERMANY Rhineland-Palatinate, Franconia

Kasseler Leberwurst

A lightly smoked, open textured pig's liver *Kochwurst*, with small pieces of ham adding texture. Marjoram and white pepper are the main flavors, with some versions including onion.

MEAT

TYPE Cooked

TYPICAL SIZE L: 10in (25cm), W: 2¾in (7cm)

GERMANY Throughout

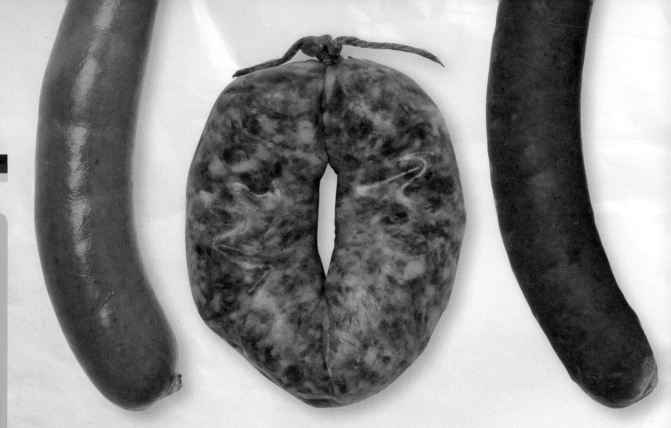

Knackwurst

A short, plump Frankfurter-style *Brühwurst* sausage made from finely ground pork and beef. It is well spiced with pepper or garlic, smoked, and scalded. It is excellent eaten with a sweet German mustard.

MEAT 🐖 and 🐖

TYPE Cooked

TYPICAL SIZE L: 6in (15cm), W: 1½in (4cm)

GERMANY Western federal states

Kohlwurst

This fairly soft *Rohwurst* sausage is made from pork, pork fat, and lungs, and strongly flavored with marjoram, thyme, mustard seeds, and allspice, then heavily smoked for 1–2 weeks. Usually warmed and eaten with kale.

MEAT 🐖

TYPE Cured and dried

TYPICAL SIZE L: 6in (15cm), W: 1in (3cm)

GERMANY Lower Saxony

Krakauer

Named after the city Kraków in Poland, this is a hot-smoked *Brühwurst* sausage that came to Germany with Polish refugees. It contains chunks of lean pork and has a punchy flavor dominated by garlic. This cooked sausage is partly dried and is eaten cold, or grilled.

MEAT 🐖

TYPE Cooked

TYPICAL SIZE L: 6¼in (16cm), W: 1½in (4cm)

GERMANY South

Landjäger

A slim *Rohwurst* sausage made from beef and pork, flavored with wine, caraway seeds, and garlic. It is pressed into a square shape between wooden boards, then smoked and dried.

MEAT 🐖 and 🐖

TYPE Cured and dried

TYPICAL SIZE L: 6in (15cm),
W: 1 x ½in (3 x 1cm)

GERMANY Swabia, Baden-Württemberg

Leberkäse

Bavarian leberkäse is a *Brühwurst* made from beef, pork, and onions (but no liver), finely ground and baked into a loaf. In Thuringia and Saxony, it must contain some liver. Many variations exist.

MEAT 🐖 and 🐖

TYPE Cooked

TYPICAL SIZE L: 12in (30cm),
W: 4 x 3in (10 x 8cm)

GERMANY Throughout, especially Bavaria and southern regions

Lyoner Fleischwurst

A good-quality Bologna-type *Brühwurst* made from cured pork. After being stuffed into the casing, it is often tied into a ring. Many variations include colorful additions such as pistachio or red peppers.

MEAT 🐖

TYPE Cooked

TYPICAL SIZE L: 12in (30cm),
W: 4in (10cm)

GERMANY Throughout

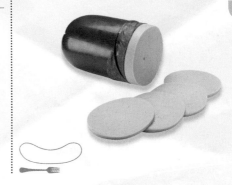

Mettwurst

Made from pork and beef, this soft *Rohwurst* is strongly flavored with paprika, nutmeg, and sugar, and then cured and smoked. It is eaten raw. In northern Germany, Mettwurst is drier and harder.

Milzwurst

A pale *Brühwurst* made from veal and pork. The stuffing is speckled with pieces of spleen, and sometimes of veal, or other offal. It is sliced and either eaten cold or fried in bread crumbs.

Möppkenbrot

The stuffing in this *Kochwurst* is made from pig's blood, rind, and rye meal, studded with back fat. The proportion of rye is so high that the consistency is almost like bread, hence the name and the typical loaf shape.

MEAT	and
TYPE	Cured
TYPICAL SIZE	L: 4in (10cm), W: 2in (5cm)
GERMANY	Throughout

MEAT	and
TYPE	Cooked
TYPICAL SIZE	L: 12in (30cm), W: 3in (8cm)
GERMANY	Bavaria

MEAT	
TYPE	Cooked
TYPICAL SIZE	L: 7in (18cm), W: 2½ x 3in (6 x 8cm)
GERMANY	Westphalia

24

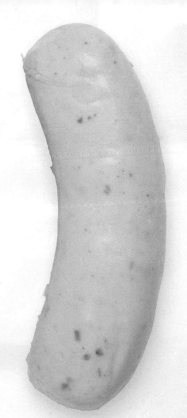

Münchner Weisswurst

A delicate, smooth *Brühwurst* made from veal and back fat, speckled with herbs. It is traditionally eaten before noon, usually for breakfast with pretzels, and the connoisseur sucks it out of its skin.

MEAT and

TYPE Cooked

TYPICAL SIZE L: 5in (12cm), W: 1in (3cm)

GERMANY Munich, Bavaria

Nürnberger Rostbratwurst PGI

Short and thin as a finger, this popular pork *Bratwurst* is flavored mainly with marjoram; other spices vary. Normally grilled, it can also be simmered in spiced vinegar.

MEAT

TYPE Cooked or fresh

TYPICAL SIZE L: 3in (8cm), W: ¾in (2cm)

GERMANY Nuremberg, Bavaria

Pfälzer Bratwurst

Coarsely chopped pork shoulder and belly is well seasoned with fresh garlic, coriander, and nutmeg, and kneaded with sparkling water. The fresh version is grilled, the cooked one sliced.

MEAT

TYPE Fresh or cooked

TYPICAL SIZE L: 5in (14cm), W: 1in (3cm)

GERMANY Palatinate

Small *Rohwurst*, such as this Pfefferwurst, are often found in Germany's mountain states, where they are popular snacks with hikers.

Germany's cooked sausages range from spreadable *Kochwurst*, such as leberwurst, to mild *Brühwurst* made for slicing or cooking.

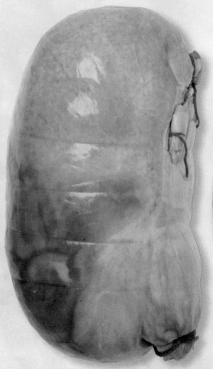

Pfälzer Saumagen

This large, broad, and bulbous *Kochwurst* is made from pork, potatoes, carrots, herbs, and spices that are all stuffed into a pig's stomach and then cooked. The skin is left on and eaten as part of the dish.

Pfefferwurst

Usually made from beef and pork, this *Rohwurst* is powerfully flavored with peppercorns and sage, and includes cumin seeds as a digestive. It is smoked over smoldering peppercorns and dried.

Pressack

A head cheese (*Sülzwurst*). The white version has large chunks of meat and skin from the pig's head, cooked in the stomach or bladder. The red version includes blood and sometimes tongue.

MEAT

TYPE Cooked

TYPICAL SIZE L: 12in (30cm), W: 6in (15cm)

GERMANY Palatinate

MEAT and

TYPE Cured and dried

TYPICAL SIZE L: 7in (18cm), W: 1in (2.5cm)

GERMANY Sauerland, Westphalia

MEAT

TYPE Cooked

TYPICAL SIZE L: 14in (36cm), W: 4in (10cm)

GERMANY Franconia, Bavaria

Regensburger

This is a short, plump, fully scalded sausage of the Frankfurter type, but with a little more texture. This *Brühwurst* is made from coarsely minced pork and beef studded with small pieces of fat and then cold smoked.

MEAT 🐄 and 🐖	
TYPE Cooked	
TYPICAL SIZE L: 3in (8cm), W: 1½in (4cm)	
GERMANY Regensburg, Bavaria	

Schwarzwurst

A dark, black pig's blood sausage, with pork, fat, bread crumbs, and onions, this *Kochwurst* is well seasoned with garlic, thyme, cloves, and nutmeg. It is cooked, then made into links, dried, and smoked.

MEAT 🐖	
TYPE Cooked	
TYPICAL SIZE L: 12in (30cm), W: 1½in (4cm)	
GERMANY Swabia	

Speckwurst

A *Kochwurst* blood sausage flavored with onions and marjoram. The sausage mixture is so liberally studded with smoked back fat that it appears as pale as a white sausage. This sausage is eaten cold as well as hot.

MEAT 🐖	
TYPE Cooked	
TYPICAL SIZE L: 10in (25cm), W: 1½in (4cm)	
GERMANY Throughout	

29

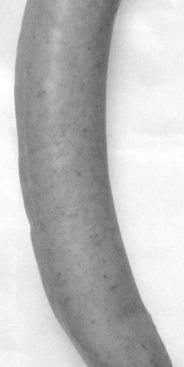

Teewurst

This is a high-quality spreadable *Rohwurst* sausage made from finely or coarsely minced pork and beef, smoked over beech and matured for 7–10 days. Eaten raw, the high fat content makes it easy to spread.

MEAT 🐖 and 🐄	
TYPE	Cured
TYPICAL SIZE	L: 8in (20cm), W: 1½in (4cm)
GERMANY	Throughout

Thüringer Rostbratwurst PGI

A long, thin *Bratwurst* sausage made from pork and beef, or sometimes veal. It is about 25 percent fat, and its distinctive spices include caraway, garlic, and marjoram. Usually grilled.

MEAT 🐖 and 🐄	
TYPE	Cooked or fresh
TYPICAL SIZE	L: 7in (18cm), W: 1in (2.5cm)
GERMANY	Thuringia

Thüringer Rotwurst PGI

This *Kochwurst* blood sausage is attractively studded with large cubes of lean and fat pork, and a little pig's liver, flavored with onion and marjoram. It is eaten both cold and hot.

MEAT 🐖	
TYPE	Cooked
TYPICAL SIZE	L: 8in (20cm), W: 2½in (6cm)
GERMANY	Thuringia

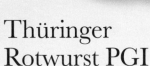

Wollwurst

A white *Brühwurst* made from finely minced veal or pork that is not stuffed into skins, but piped directly into simmering water. This gives them their characteristic "woolly" surface. They are eaten at once, or fried until golden.

MEAT or

TYPE Cooked

TYPICAL SIZE L: 6in (15cm), W: 1in (3cm)

GERMANY Bavaria

Zervelatwurst

Also spelled *Cervelatwurst*, this is a popular smoked *Rohwurst* sausage with a delicate flavor. Made from finely ground beef, pork, back fat, pepper, and brandy, it is served thinly sliced.

MEAT and

TYPE Cured and dried

TYPICAL SIZE L: 16in (40cm), W: 2in (5cm)

GERMANY Throughout

Zungenwurst

Large pieces of pork, skin, fat, and especially tongue, are attractively arranged and bound together with pig's blood, oatmeal, bread crumbs, and suet, in a large brawn *Kochwurst* sausage. Sliced and eaten cold.

MEAT

TYPE Cooked

TYPICAL SIZE L: 10in (25cm), W: 4in (10cm)

GERMANY Throughout

AUSTRIA

Although Vienna boasts highly sophisticated pastry cooks, outside the capital Austrian food is more rustic, featuring hearty, starchy, and fatty delights. Sausages fit this profile perfectly, so not surprisingly, the *würstelstand* is a much-frequented feature of any town center. The best place to sample sausages in traditional Austrian cuisine is at a *gasthaus*: a simple restaurant serving regional food.

In terms of flavor, Austria is at the meeting point of Eastern and Western Europe, so Hungarian, Czech, German, and Italian influences can be found in the variety of styles, spices, and names of its sausages. Their manufacturing is strictly regulated, and mechanically recovered meat is not permitted. Austria shares with Germany the classifications of *Rohwurst* and *Brühwurst* (see page 14). And one cannot leave Austria without mentioning the most famous sausage in the world —the *Wiener Würstel* or Frankfurter—which was invented by Johann Georg Lahner, a Frankfurt butcher, when he settled in Vienna.

Bergsalami

Made in Austria's mountain regions, this is a fine-grained pork *Rohwurst* that is cured, then hot smoked over beech chippings and juniper. It is dried for up to six weeks to produce the characteristic white mold on its skin.

MEAT 🐖

TYPE Cured and dried

TYPICAL SIZE L: 12in (30cm), W: 2½in (6cm)

AUSTRIA Burgenland and Styria

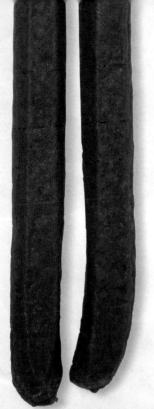

Debreziner

A long, slim *Brühwurst* made from mixed pork and beef, filled into a narrow sheep's casing, then scalded in boiling water and smoked to a golden brown. Flavored with paprika, it comes in either mild or hot-and-spicy versions.

MEAT and

TYPE Cooked

TYPICAL SIZE L: 10in (25cm), W: ¾in (2cm)

AUSTRIA Throughout

Dürre im Kranz

Dark and wrinkled, this *Brühwurst* is made from lean beef and pork, speckled with small pieces of fat and herbs, then formed into a ring, scalded, smoked, and dried. It is eaten cold, sliced.

MEAT and

TYPE Cooked

TYPICAL SIZE L: 13in (34cm), W: 1½in (4cm)

AUSTRIA Throughout, especially Vienna

Extrawurst

Beef, pork, and bacon are minced to a paste and seasoned with pepper and garlic, then scalded. This *Brühwurst* is served cold, very thinly sliced. *Feine Extrawurst* is an even smoother version.

MEAT and

TYPE Cooked

TYPICAL SIZE L: 10in (25cm), W: 4in (10cm)

AUSTRIA Throughout

33

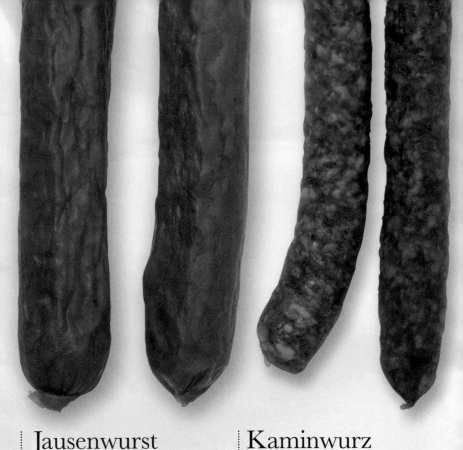

Jagdsalami

This sausage is dried, and was originally taken out by hunters as a snack, as it is firm and easy to transport. A *Rohwurst* sausage made from beef and pork, it is flavored with pepper and garlic and often pressed into a square section.

MEAT and

TYPE Cured and dried

TYPICAL SIZE L: 10in (25cm), W: 2 x 2in (5 x 5cm)

AUSTRIA Tyrol

Jausenwurst

This is a mild-flavored, medium-grained *Brühwurst*. Made from seasoned beef, lean pork, and back fat, the mixture is bound with potato starch, then scalded and smoked over beechwood. It is eaten cold.

MEAT and

TYPE Cooked

TYPICAL SIZE L: 6in (15cm), W: 1in (3cm)

AUSTRIA Throughout

Kaminwurz

Beef (or sometimes venison or goat) and pork are flavored with mountain herbs such as thyme, sage, hyssop, and juniper. The name comes from "camino" or fireplace, where this *Rohwurst* is double smoked.

MEAT and

TYPE Cured and dried

TYPICAL SIZE L: 4½in (11cm), W: ½in (1cm)

AUSTRIA Tyrol

Kantwurst

This pork and beef *Rohwurst* is pressed between boards to form its characteristic square shape. Flavored with ginger, coriander, caraway, and garlic, it is dried for up to six weeks.

 MEAT and

TYPE Cured and dried

TYPICAL SIZE L: 16in (40cm), W: 2½ x 1½in (6 x 4cm)

AUSTRIA Tyrol

Kärtner Hauswürstel

A country-style, rustic *Rohwurst* made from pork, beef, and fat, that is well seasoned with pepper and garlic before being smoked and then dried. The texture can be coarse or medium.

 MEAT and

TYPE Cured and dried

TYPICAL SIZE L: 8½in (22cm), W: 1in (3.5cm)

AUSTRIA Throughout, especially Carinthia

Käsekreiner

A smooth-textured *Brühwurst* studded with chunks of Emmental cheese (hence its name) that melt unctuously when the sausage is grilled. It is a popular street food, served hot in crusty bread with spicy mustard.

 MEAT

TYPE Cooked

TYPICAL SIZE L: 6in (15cm), W: ¾in (2cm)

AUSTRIA Throughout

Mährische

A medium-grained Moravian *Brühwurst* smade from lean pork, beef, back fat, and green peppercorns. It is cooked, smoked, and dried. Served with pickled cabbage or made into soup.

 MEAT 🐷 and 🐗

TYPE Cooked

TYPICAL SIZE L: 10in (25cm), W: 3in (8cm)

AUSTRIA Throughout Lower Austria

Paprika Fleischwurst

A pale, smooth-textured *Brühwurst* that has flecks of chiles that give it a speckled appearance. Similar to Hungarian *csabai kolbász*, it is flavored with sweet paprika. It is sliced and eaten cold.

 MEAT 🐷

TYPE Cooked

TYPICAL SIZE L: 16in (40cm), W: 4in (10cm)

AUSTRIA Throughout

Salzburger

A mild *Brühwurst* sausage made from beef and pork back fat, bound with potato starch. Similar to a Frankfurter, it is then lightly scalded and sometimes smoked. It is simmered again before eating.

 MEAT 🐷 and 🐷

TYPE Cooked

TYPICAL SIZE L: 5in (13cm), W: 1in (3cm)

AUSTRIA Salzburg

36

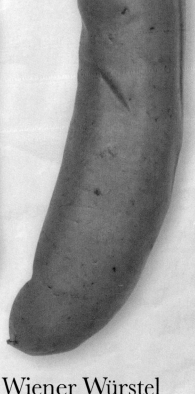

Tiroler

A smooth, pink *Brühwurst* sausage containing mainly lean cured pork with a little veal added and sometimes beef as well. It is nicely mottled with coarse chunks of fat throughout to add moisture. It is sliced and eaten cold.

 MEAT 🐖 and 🐄
___
TYPE Cooked
___
TYPICAL SIZE L: 5in (13cm), W: 2in (5cm)
___
AUSTRIA Tyrol

Ungarische Salami

As its name suggests, this is a fine-grained *Rohwurst* with a typical Hungarian spicing of that country's favorite flavoring: paprika. It is air dried for six weeks, which produces an attractive white mold on the skin.

 MEAT 🐖
___
TYPE Cured and dried
___
TYPICAL SIZE L: 16in (40cm), W: 2½in (6cm)
___
AUSTRIA Throughout, especially Burgenland

Wiener Würstel

The original Frankfurter was first created in Vienna. Invented by a butcher from Frankfurt, this *Brühwurst* is made from pork, beef, and pork back fat, and is lightly smoked. *Sacherwürstel* is a longer, luxury version.

 MEAT 🐖 and 🐄
___
TYPE Cooked
___
TYPICAL SIZE L: 7in (17cm), W: ¾in (2cm)
___
AUSTRIA Throughout, especially Vienna

SWITZERLAND

Switzerland's stunning mountain scenery dominates every view, and its alpine pastures are the source of many of her best-loved products. Traditional Swiss food is rustic and regional, as might be expected from a nation of farmers. There is a strong organic and biodynamic movement, and feeling part of nature is important to many Swiss families. The tiny eating places nestling halfway up a steep vineyard or carved into caves provide seasonal and regional food that is well worth seeking out.

Switzerland may be most famous for cheese and chocolate, but it is also a land of sausages. Like its southern neighbors, sausages are regionally based with each canton having its own specialities. These tend to reflect the styles of the nearest neighboring country, be it Germany, France, or Italy. As a result, there is a wonderful range of dried mountain sausages, fresh sausages, cooked, cured, smoked, and scalded sausages to savor.

Appenzeller Knoblauch Pantli

A *Rohwurst* made from beef, pork, back fat, pepper, wine, and garlic, the last being the dominant flavor. The sausages are cured in a square press for up to 10 days before being dried and smoked.

MEAT and

TYPE Cured and dried

TYPICAL SIZE L: 6–8in (15–20cm), W: 1 x ¾in (3 x 2cm)

SWITZERLAND Appenzell

Berner Zungenwurst

Despite its name, this *Brühwurst* is not made from tongue but from pork, beef, and back fat, flavored with mace, nutmeg, coriander, and cumin. It is cold smoked for 6–7 days before being cooked. It is usually eaten cold.

MEAT	and
TYPE	Cooked
TYPICAL SIZE	L: 8in (20cm), W: 2in (5cm)
SWITZERLAND	Bern

Boutefas AOC

A lightly smoked *Rohwurst* whose bulbous shape comes from the pig's stomach used as a casing. Made from the pork of fat Vaudois pigs, it is flavored with garlic, coriander, and white wine, and then cured. Traditionally it was always cooked, but nowadays it is also sliced and served raw.

MEAT	
TYPE	Cured and part-dried
TYPICAL SIZE	L: 6in (15cm), W: 4½in (11cm)
SWITZERLAND	Vaud

Cervelas

Considered by some as the Swiss national sausage, this thick, short *Brühwurst* is traditionally stuffed into zebu beef casings. Made from finely minced pork and beef, it is briefly smoked, then scalded. It is cut into cubes and served with cheese, or grilled with the ends slashed, so they open out.

MEAT	and
TYPE	Cooked
TYPICAL SIZE	L: 5in (12cm), W: 1½in (4cm)
SWITZERLAND	Throughout

39

Emmentalerli

Despite its name, this coarse-grained, peppery pork *Brühwurst* does not contain cheese. Lightly smoked, it is simmered or grilled, and forms part of a *Berner Platte*: a platter of bacon, ham, and sausages, served with sauerkraut and green beans.

MEAT 🐖

TYPE Cooked

TYPICAL SIZE L: 6½in (17cm), W: ¾in (2cm)

SWITZERLAND Emmental

Grisoni

A small, dried *Rohwurst* sausage very popular with hikers. It is characterized by the white mold on the surface. Made from beef with pork and back fat, it is cured in a square press and dried for up to a month. It is sometimes eaten with potatoes and melted cheese.

MEAT 🐄 and 🐖

TYPE Cured and dried

TYPICAL SIZE L: 6in (15cm), W: 2 x 2in (5 x 5cm)

SWITZERLAND Grisons

Salametti

Like its Italian counterpart, this is a *Rohwurst*. Small and plump, it is usually made from beef and pork, but occasionally contains horse meat. Well flavored with pepper and sometimes wine, it is a popular snack sausage.

MEAT 🐄 and 🐖

TYPE Cured and dried

TYPICAL SIZE L: 3½in (9cm), W: 1in (2.5cm)

SWITZERLAND Throughout, especially Italian border regions

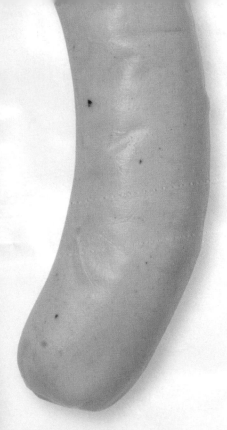

Sankt Galler Bratwurst PGI

Originally known as Olma-Bratwurst, this delicate, scalded sausage is made from finely minced veal and pork, moistened with milk and flavored with mace. It is grilled or fried, but is not traditionally served with mustard.

MEAT	and
TYPE	Cooked
TYPICAL SIZE	L: 8in (20cm), W: 1in (2.5cm)
SWITZERLAND	St. Gallen

Saucisson Vaudois PGI

A short, irregular-shaped *Rohwurst,* this pork sausage is cured and cold smoked. It is usually cooked and eaten hot, but some versions are dried and eaten raw. There is another version that includes white cabbage.

MEAT	
TYPE	Cured, or cured and dried
TYPICAL SIZE	L: 6½in (17cm), W: 2¾in (7cm)
SWITZERLAND	Vaud

Waadtländer Bratwurst

Coarsely minced fresh pork is flavored with nutmeg, mace, marjoram, and white wine. Then it is either formed into portion-sized segments, or coiled into a spiral. It is usually grilled, but is sometimes boiled first.

MEAT	
TYPE	Fresh
TYPICAL SIZE	L: 6in (15cm), W: 1in (3cm)
SWITZERLAND	Vaud

41

FRANCE

Bordering Spain, Italy, and Germany, the diversity of French sausages reflects these major sausage-making neighbors. The pride with which France regards its regional specialities is demonstrated by the many colorful _confréries_ which have an annual parade and dinner to champion and promote their local sausage.

Northern France tends towards scalded or slicing sausages of the German type, and hearty tripe sausages. Nearer the Pyrenees, there are similarities to Spain, such as the tradition of eating sausages with snails. In the Alps of eastern France, there is a wealth of dried sausages which, like many Italian salamis, are not fermented but tend to be simply spiced with salt and pepper. In some central and southern areas that used to be very impoverished, there are fascinating examples of sausages bulked out with seasonal vegetables instead of meat. In contrast, sumptuous sausages including champagne, _foie gras_, or truffles, exist for the wealthier epicure.

Andouille

Made from pig's tripe and intestines cut into strips and brined, the strips are rolled and stuffed into a large skin and cooked. Sometimes it is smoked. It is sliced thinly and eaten cold.

MEAT 🐖

TYPE Cooked

TYPICAL SIZE L: 12in (30cm), W: 2¾in (7cm)

FRANCE Throughout, especially Normandy

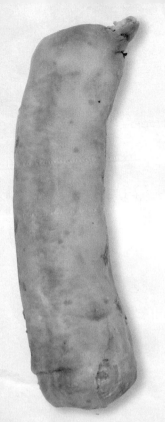

Andouillette

A rustic, unsmoked sausage made with large sheets of tripe and pork, andouillette is usually grilled and eaten hot with mustard. It has a pungent and distinctive aroma. Those made by members of the AAAAA (*Association Amicale des Amateurs d'Andouillette Authentique*) are the best; the association is based in Troyes.

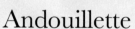

MEAT 🐖	
TYPE Cooked	
TYPICAL SIZE L: 6in (15cm), W: 1in (1cm)	
FRANCE Throughout, especially Troyes	

Boudin blanc

A delicate white sausage made with finely pounded veal, chicken, rabbit, or other white meat, subtly seasoned with fresh herbs. It often includes luxury additions such as cream, chestnuts, truffles, or fungi.

MEAT 🐑 and 🐓	
TYPE Cooked	
TYPICAL SIZE L: 5in (12cm), W: 1in (3cm)	
FRANCE Throughout	

Boudin noir

A light-textured blood sausage including chunks of pork skin and meat. Regional varieties contain cream, spinach, onion, or chestnuts. Made into coils or links, it is fried and served with apple. Although now made all year round, it was traditionally made in January.

MEAT 🐖	
TYPE Cooked	
TYPICAL SIZE L: 39in (1 meter), W: 1in (3cm)	
FRANCE Throughout	

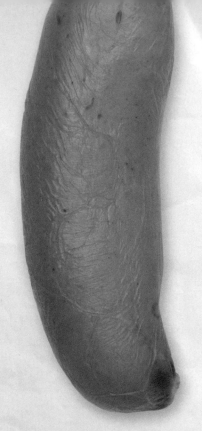
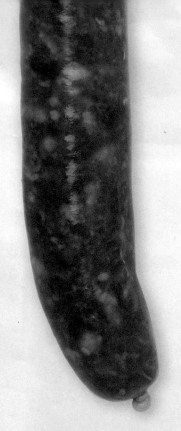

Cervelas

This short, plump, cooked sausage resembles its Swiss namesake. It is made from pork, or pork and beef, with garlic, coriander, allspice, and nutmeg. It is poached in red wine or water, or eaten cold, sliced, or cubed. When eaten cold, it is served with cheese.

MEAT 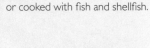 and	
TYPE Cooked	
TYPICAL SIZE L: 5in (12cm), W: 1½in (4cm)	
FRANCE Alsace	

Chipolata

Long, finger-width sausages, generally made from lean pork and pork fat, though chipolata-style sausages can be made from other meats. Spices vary according to the maker. They are fried, grilled, or served as part of a garnish.

MEAT	
TYPE Fresh	
TYPICAL SIZE L: 7in (18cm), W: ¾in (2cm)	
FRANCE Throughout	

Chorizo Basquais

Similar in character to Spanish chorizo, this version from the Basque country is softer and less spicy than many. It is often added to dishes, such as the famous *Poulet Basquaise*, or cooked with fish and shellfish.

MEAT	
TYPE Cured and dried	
TYPICAL SIZE L: 14in (36cm), W: 2in (5cm)	
FRANCE Pyrenees	

Cou de canard farcie

Hashed duck meat and chunks of *foie gras* are salted, stuffed into the neck skin, and cooked. Deluxe versions include truffles, cheaper versions include pork. Sliced and eaten cold or hot.

MEAT 🦆 and 🐷	
TYPE Cooked	
TYPICAL SIZE L: 6in (15cm), W: 2¾in (7cm)	
FRANCE Périgord	

Crepinette

Also called *fricandeau*, these are round patties of well-seasoned pork or veal sausage, wrapped in caul fat. They are sold both cooked and ready to eat, or uncooked for grilling or baking.

MEAT 🐷 or 🐑	
TYPE Fresh or cooked	
TYPICAL SIZE L: 5in (12cm), W: 2¾ x ¾in (7 x 2cm)	
FRANCE Throughout	

Diot fumé

A pork sausage flavored with nutmeg and garlic. Some include seasonal vegetables, such as leeks, cabbage, or beets, and they can be dried or smoked. They are traditionally simmered in white wine and onions.

MEAT 🐷	
TYPE Cured and dried	
TYPICAL SIZE L: 6in (15cm), W: 1in (3cm)	
FRANCE Savoy	

Figatelli

A slim, wrinkled pork sausage made from liver and blood, with small cubes of fat. It is lightly smoked, and can be quite hard. It is eaten raw and sliced, but is also cooked in dishes. *Figatellu* is the Corsican spelling.

MEAT

TYPE Dried

TYPICAL SIZE L: 8in (20cm), W: 1in (3cm)

FRANCE Corsica

Gendarme

A rectangular sectioned sausage made from beef, pork skin, and pork fat, strongly seasoned with peppery spices and wine, then highly smoked, dried, and pressed. They are often sold in pairs.

MEAT and

TYPE Cured and dried

TYPICAL SIZE L: 6¼in (16cm), W: ½ × 1in (1.5 × 3cm)

FRANCE Alsace and Jura

Jésus de Lyon

So called because its plump shape resembles a swaddled baby. A large, coarsely chopped, pure pork sausage studded with large pieces of fat. It is dried and served thinly sliced. The curious shape is formed by the pig's stomach into which the meat is stuffed.

MEAT

TYPE Dried

TYPICAL SIZE L: 10in (26cm), W: 6in (15cm)

FRANCE Lyon, Rhône-Alpes

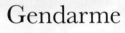

Knack

These smoked Alsace sausages are made from pork and beef, so are darker pink than Frankfurters. Their name comes from the sound they made when they burst open. They are eaten with *choucroûte* or boiled potatoes, and, naturally, mustard.

MEAT 🐷 and 🐄

TYPE Cooked

TYPICAL SIZE L: 6½in (17cm), W: ¾in (2cm)

FRANCE Alsace and Franche-Comté

Merguez

Brought to France from its North African colonies, this popular, spicy red sausage is made from lamb or beef, and strongly flavored with paprika. It can be fresh or dried.

MEAT 🐑 or 🐷

TYPE Fresh or dried

TYPICAL SIZE L: 6in (15cm), W: ¾in (2cm)

FRANCE Throughout

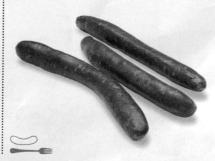

Mettwurst

This is a very smooth pork pâté that is stuffed into large sausage casings and cooked. Its high fat content gives it an exceptionally fine texture. It is eaten as a *tartine*: spread on toast or a cracker.

MEAT 🐷

TYPE Cooked

TYPICAL SIZE L: 6½in (17cm), W: 1½in (4cm)

FRANCE Alsace and Franche-Comté

47

Such is the fame of *saucissons secs* that they are even found in foreign markets. The floury white coating is a sign of maturation.

Market stalls in France feature a dazzling variety of *saucissons secs*, with flavors ranging from smoked pork (pictured here) to ostrich.

Montbéliard

A plump, smoked, cooked sausage flavored with garlic, cumin, and nutmeg, it is one of the three sausages used for an authentic *choucrôute garnie*. It is also eaten with warm *cancoillote* cheese, which is spreadable and comes in a jar.

MEAT	🐷
TYPE	Cooked
TYPICAL SIZE	L: 7in (18cm), W: 1in (3cm)
FRANCE	Franche-Comté

Rosette de Lyon

From the gastronomic center of France, Lyon's most famous sausage is called *rosette* because of its pink color. Made from pork shoulder with a high fat content, it is slowly matured and served thinly sliced. There are similar *rosettes* made in other regions, such as *Rosette de Bourgogne*.

MEAT	🐷
TYPE	Dried
TYPICAL SIZE	L: 20in (50cm), W: 2in (5.5cm)
FRANCE	Lyon, Rhône-Alpes

Saucisse de canard

A common by-product of the *foie gras* and *magret de canard* industry, the best are labeled "*pur canard.*" Cheaper versions are mixed with pork. They are usually slim sausages, sold fresh for grilling. As well as the Périgord, the areas around Strasbourg and Brittany are big duck-producing areas.

MEAT	🦆
TYPE	Fresh
TYPICAL SIZE	L: 6in (15cm), W: ¾in (2cm)
FRANCE	Throughout, especially the Périgord

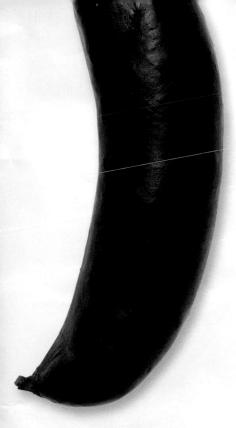

Saucisse de cheval

Made from horse meat, these sausages are darker and leaner than pork or beef. They come in a variety of forms, either fresh for grilling, or else cured and cooked, when they are recooked or sliced and eaten cold.

MEAT 🐎

TYPE Fresh or cooked

TYPICAL SIZE L: 8in (20cm), W: 2in (5cm)

FRANCE Throughout

Saucisse de lapin

Most rabbit eaten in France is domestic, and because they have a more delicate flavor than wild rabbit, these sausages tend to be flavored with herbs such as thyme, rosemary, or tarragon.

MEAT 🐰

TYPE Fresh

TYPICAL SIZE L: 5½in (14cm), W: ¾in (2cm)

FRANCE Throughout

Saucisse de Morteau PGI

Flavored with garlic, shallots, cumin, coriander, and white wine, this coarse-grained sausage is smoked over pine and juniper. Normally sold uncooked, it is also sold cooked for eating cold or reheating.

MEAT 🐷

TYPE Cured or cooked

TYPICAL SIZE L: 7in (18cm), W: 2½in (6cm)

FRANCE Franche-Comté

51

Saucisse de Strasbourg

In this French version of Frankfurter, pork and fat is finely minced and seasoned with nutmeg and coriander, and then smoked. It is boiled and served as part of *choucrôute garnie*.

MEAT 🐷

TYPE Cooked

TYPICAL SIZE L: 6in (15cm), W: 1in (2.5cm)

FRANCE Alsace

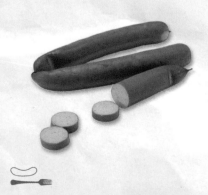

Saucisse de Toulouse

A coarsely chopped, fresh sausage made from pork shoulder, belly, and smoked ham, with a simple seasoning of salt, sugar, and white pepper. It is an essential ingredient in the famous Toulouse cassoulet.

MEAT 🐷

TYPE Fresh

TYPICAL SIZE L: 4in (10cm), W: 1in (3cm)

FRANCE Toulouse, Midi-Pyrénées

Saucisse sèche à la perche

The name comes from the stick (*perche*) over which the long lengths are hung in loops to dry. It is made from coarsely chopped lean and fat pork, and dried for 2–3 weeks. It is also known as *saucisse sèche perchée*.

MEAT 🐷

TYPE Dried

TYPICAL SIZE L: 39in (1 meter), W: 1½in (4cm)

FRANCE Ardèche and Aveyron

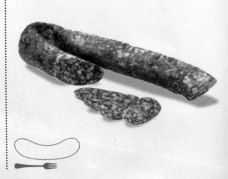

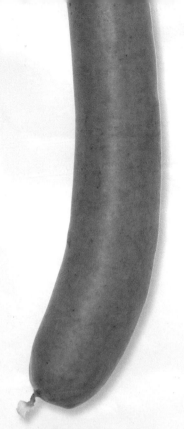

Saucisse Viennoise

A high-quality Frankfurter-style of sausage made from equal parts of veal and lean pork, seasoned with cayenne pepper and coriander. It is lightly smoked, and comes in several sizes. Like Weiner Würstel, they are simmered before eating.

MEAT 🐄 and 🐖

TYPE Cooked

TYPICAL SIZE L: 6in (15cm), W: 1in (2.5cm)

FRANCE Alsace

Saucisson sec au Beaufort

This pork sausage comes from the mountainous region of Savoy where dried meats are a speciality. Interspersed through the sausage meat are chunks of strong Beaufort cheese.

MEAT 🐖

TYPE Dried

TYPICAL SIZE L: 6in (15cm), W: 2in (5cm)

FRANCE Beaufort, Savoy (Rhône-Alpes)

Saucisson sec au poivre

Coarsely cracked black peppercorns form a thick, crunchy coating around this dried pork sausage, giving a fiery flavor to each slice. It is best thinly sliced, and served with a contrasting, white-skinned *saucisson*.

MEAT 🐖

TYPE Dried

TYPICAL SIZE L: 6in (15cm), W: 2in (5cm)

FRANCE Throughout

Saucisson sec aux herbes

This popular *saucisson* is rolled in a thick, green covering of strongly flavored dried *herbes de Provence* such as thyme, rosemary, tarragon, fennel, or marjoram. It is often served with green olives.

MEAT

TYPE Dried

TYPICAL SIZE L: 6in (15cm), W: 2in (5cm)

FRANCE Throughout, especially Provence

Saucisson sec aux noix

This version of the standard *saucisson sec* has pieces of walnut dotted throughout the pork meat and fat, giving a pleasant crunchy texture, as well as a nutty flavor. Another version uses hazelnuts (*noisettes*).

MEAT

TYPE Dried

TYPICAL SIZE L: 7in (18cm), W: 2in (5cm)

FRANCE Throughout, especially Grenoble and the Périgord

Saucisson sec d'âne

A slightly controversial salami-style sausage made from donkey meat which is dark in color. They are a common sight at French summer markets, and are mostly made for the tourist market.

MEAT

TYPE Dried

TYPICAL SIZE L: 8in (20cm), W: 2½in (6cm)

FRANCE South and Southwest

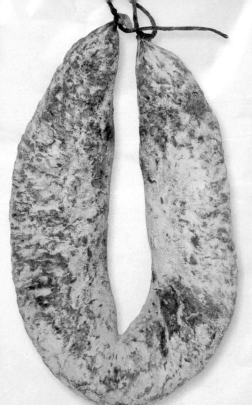

Saucisson sec de cheval

Sometimes mixed with pork fat, the meat of this sausage is dark and lean, with a strong beefy flavor. France is one of the few European countries where horse meat is still available on the high street and at markets.

MEAT

TYPE Dried

TYPICAL SIZE L: 8in (20cm), W: 3½in (9cm)

FRANCE Throughout

Saucisson sec de l'Ardèche PGI

Made from the pork of heavy-weight pigs, this dried mountain sausage comes in six different sizes, ranging from the classic cylinder to the enormous *Jésus*. Whole peppercorns are visible in the slices.

MEAT

TYPE Dried

TYPICAL SIZE L: 6¼in (16cm), W: 1½in (3.5cm)

FRANCE Ardèche

Saucisson sec de sanglier

Wild boar are common throughout the forests of France, and although the meat is rather tough for normal use, it makes extremely good *saucisson sec*. The meat is lean, well flavored, and is a deep, rich red.

MEAT

TYPE Dried

TYPICAL SIZE L: 7in (18cm), W: 1¾in (4.5cm)

FRANCE Throughout

ITALY

Italy is the birthplace of that huge and well-traveled family called salami; its history goes back more than 2,000 years. There are two categories: *salame crudo* (raw salami) which is dried and eaten raw, and *salame cotto* (cooked salami) which is made from cheaper cuts of meat less suited to raw consumption.

An important feature of Italian salami is that it can be made without the curing salt used by many other countries. This is because their pork comes from heavy-weight pigs that are grown for much longer than normal commercial pigs, and whose composition is such that their pork can be safely matured using only salt. Since many Italian salamis have only pepper and perhaps garlic added, this gives them a very pure taste.

Sausages from the poorer south tend to include pungent herbs and vegetables, such as chiles, wild fennel, and garlic. In northern Italy, the traditionally more expensive spices such as black pepper, cloves, and cinnamon prevail, and the locals there also tend to slice their hard-dried salami paper-thin.

Buristo

A plump black sausage cooked in the pig's stomach or made into links. Including the rind, head meat, and fat, it is flavored with ingredients such as lemon, garlic, parsley, pine nuts, cinnamon, and raisins. It has a soft texture.

MEAT	
TYPE Cooked	
TYPICAL SIZE L: 10in (25cm), W: 3in (7.5cm)	
ITALY Tuscany	

Capocollo

Pork necks or shoulders are salted and massaged with wine vinegar, and stuffed into large skins with whole peppercorns and garlic, bound with twine and reeds, then slowly dried.

Cotechino Modena PGI

Pork rind is mixed with lean pork and fat, finely ground, and stuffed into natural pork casings. The salami is then cooked and dried in ovens. It is eaten hot.

Finocchiona

Wild fennel grows all over Tuscany, and it is the cracked seeds with black pepper that give this salami its powerful flavor. Some versions of Finocchiona are rolled in dried fennel leaves.

MEAT

TYPE Dried

TYPICAL SIZE L: 10in (25cm), W: 2¾in (7cm)

ITALY Central and southern Italy

MEAT

TYPE Cooked

TYPICAL SIZE L: 8in (20cm), W: 3in (8cm)

ITALY Modena, Emilia Romagna

MEAT

TYPE Dried

TYPICAL SIZE L: 10in (25cm), W: 3in (8cm)

ITALY Tuscany

57

Luganega

A fresh sausage that is coiled and not linked, and is sold by length. Many flavors exist including cloves and cinnamon, herbs, lightly smoked, citrus, or wine. This sausage is used in many recipes. As well as frying and grilling, it can be used in stews or crumbled and added to pasta.

MEAT 🐖

TYPE Fresh

TYPICAL SIZE L: 39in (1 meter), W: 1in (2.5cm)

ITALY Throughout, especially the northeast

Mortadella Bologna PGI

Made from finely pounded pork studded with cubes of fat and carefully cooked, mortadella comes in many sizes, the largest more than 220lb (100kg). It should be sliced paper-thin.

MEAT 🐖

TYPE Cooked

TYPICAL SIZE L: 12in (30cm), W: 5in (12cm)

ITALY Bologna, Emilia Romagna

'Nduja

Made from offcuts of pork including the offal and cheek, 'nduja is quite brightly colored and powerfully seasoned with red chiles. This type of sausage has a soft, spreadable consistency. It is usually simply spread on bread.

MEAT 🐖

TYPE Cured

TYPICAL SIZE L: 8in (20cm), W: 3in (8cm)

ITALY Spilinga, Calabria

58

Salame al Barolo

As its name suggests, this short, medium-grained salami from Piedmont is made from pork that is seasoned with Barolo, a full-bodied red wine. It is matured for 2–4 weeks.

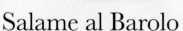

MEAT 🐖	
TYPE Dried	
TYPICAL SIZE L: 10in (25cm) W: 2in (5cm)	
ITALY Piedmont	

Salame al tartufo

This fine-grained salami is delicately seasoned and sometimes includes white wine. Its high fat content absorbs the aromas of the fragrant pieces of black or white truffles. Either version commands a high price.

MEAT 🐖 and 🐗	
TYPE Dried	
TYPICAL SIZE L: 8in (20cm), W: 2in (5cm)	
ITALY Umbria, Emilia Romagna, and Piedmont	

Salame Brianza PDO

A deep red, hard salami flavored with wine, sugar, garlic, and peppercorns, and studded with white fat. It is made in both fine-grained and coarse-grained versions.

MEAT 🐖	
TYPE Dried	
TYPICAL SIZE L: 12in (30cm), W: 3in (7.5cm)	
ITALY Brianza, Lombardy	

Salame cacciatore PDO

Mild flavored and not too salty, with only pepper and garlic as flavorings, "cacciatore" refers to the hunter who puts this salami (or the smaller salamini) in his pocket.

MEAT 🐷

TYPE Dried

TYPICAL SIZE L: 6in (15cm), W: 1½in (4cm)

ITALY Central and northern Italy

Salame ciauscolo PGI

A pale, soft salami made from lean pork and belly fat, with black pepper, wine, and garlic. It is cured, lightly smoked, and matured. It is eaten spread on to bread.

MEAT 🐷

TYPE Cured

TYPICAL SIZE L: 12in (30cm), W: 3in (8cm)

ITALY The Marches

Salame Cremona PGI

With its uniform balance of meat to fat, this salami is bound with strings that give an irregular slice. Slow maturation in the humid Po valley produces its aromatic flavor.

MEAT 🐷

TYPE Dried

TYPICAL SIZE L: 8in (20cm), W: 3in (7.5cm)

ITALY Cremona, Lombardy; also Piedmont, Veneto, and Emilia Romagna

Salame di cinghiale

Wild boar damage crops and vineyards, so throughout the winter they are pursued by hunters. Their meat is leaner and darker than pork, giving the salami a rich flavor.

MEAT 🐗

TYPE Dried

TYPICAL SIZE L: 8in (20cm), W: 1½in (4cm)

ITALY Throughout, especially Tuscany and Umbria

Salame di Felino PGI

This coarse-grained salami has less fat and more lean pork than most. Flavored with garlic and white wine, it is long and narrow, and is traditionally sliced diagonally.

MEAT 🐖

TYPE Dried

TYPICAL SIZE L: 16in (40cm), W: 1½in (4cm)

ITALY Felino and Parma, Emilia Romagna

Salame di Varzi PDO

Originally prepared for nobility, this salami is made from top-quality pork with garlic and red wine, tied with twine, and dried. The different sizes are dried for up to six months.

MEAT 🐖

TYPE Dried

TYPICAL SIZE L: 10in (25cm), W: 3in (8cm)

ITALY Pavia, Lombardy

61

Salame d'oca

Goose fat and liver are mixed with fatty pork, and traditionally stuffed into the skin of a goose neck. Then the salami is dried and cooked. Soft and mottled pink, it is served with *mostarda*—fruits pickled in mustard seeds—which cuts through the fat.

MEAT 🦢 and 🐖

TYPE Cooked

TYPICAL SIZE L: 6in (15cm), W: 2½in (6cm)

ITALY Pavia, Lombardy

Salame Milano

This internationally known pork and beef salami is fine grained with a texture that is soft, and comprises a mild seasoning of sea salt and red wine. It is dried for 3 to 6 months. In Milan, it is enjoyed simply on *michetta*, a typical Milanese bread, without any condiments.

MEAT 🐖 and 🐖

TYPE Dried

TYPICAL SIZE L: 8in (20cm), W: 2in (5cm)

ITALY Milan, Lombardy

Salame Napoli PDO

This usually has the robust, peppery seasoning typical of the south, but can be mild as well. It is coarse-grained, and a light smoking lends sweetness to counteract the spice.

MEAT 🐖

TYPE Dried

TYPICAL SIZE L: 16in (40cm), W: 2in (5cm)

ITALY Naples, Campania

Salame Piacentino PDO

A coarse-grained salami with a deep red color, it is matured for at least 45 days, and has a sweet but slightly spicy taste. It is tied with twine in the traditional way.

MEAT	🐖
TYPE Dried	
TYPICAL SIZE L: 7in (18cm), W: 2½in (6cm)	
ITALY Piacenza, Emilia Romagna	

Salame Sardo

A slim, pork salami flavored with garlic, herbs, and sometimes red wine, this gets its fiery kick from red-hot chiles. It is often made into a rustic horseshoe shape and is delicious eaten with good-quality Sardinian pecorino cheese.

MEAT	🐖
TYPE Dried	
TYPICAL SIZE L: 13in (34cm), W: 2½in (6cm)	
ITALY Sardinia	

Salame Toscano

Made from minced pork studded with large pieces of pork fat, this is a dark red, intensely flavored, and salty salami, designed to be eaten with unsalted Tuscan bread. It is sometimes paired with figs in summer as a light starter.

MEAT	🐖
TYPE Dried	
TYPICAL SIZE L: 8in (20cm), W: 2½in (6cm)	
ITALY Tuscany	

63

Salsicce fresche

Fresh pork or beef sausage, made into links or a coil. Southern versions use herbs such as fennel, wild garlic, and chile; whereas in the north, flavorings such as pepper and nutmeg are more common.

MEAT ▮ or ▮

TYPE Fresh

TYPICAL SIZE L: 2½in (6cm), W: 1in (3cm)

ITALY Throughout

Salsiccia di Calabria PDO

Pork shoulder and ribs are flavored with hot and mild chiles, wine, garlic, and fennel seeds. They are often hand-plaited into the traditional chain. Eaten raw or used as an ingredient.

MEAT ▮

TYPE Cured and dried

TYPICAL SIZE L: 16in (40cm), W: 1in (3cm)

ITALY Calabria

Sopprèssa Veneto

The best cuts of pork are coarsely chopped and spiced with pepper, cinnamon, cloves, nutmeg, rosemary, and sometimes garlic. This sausage has a delicate flavor with very little salt. Slices of grilled polenta or the traditional sponge biscuits *pan biscotto* make a good accompaniment.

MEAT ▮

TYPE Dried

TYPICAL SIZE L: 12in (30cm), W: 3in (7.5cm)

ITALY Veneto

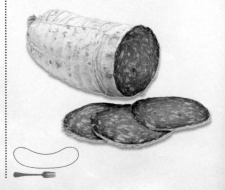

Soppressata di Calabria PDO

A flattened, orange-red sausage made from the best pork cuts with cumin, chiles, and salt. If marked *piccante* it contains hot chile, *dolce* has sweet paprika, while *bianca* contains no paprika.

MEAT 🐖

TYPE Cured and dried

TYPICAL SIZE L: 7in (18cm), W: 2 x 4in (5 x 10cm)

ITALY Calabria

Spianata di Calabria

Finely minced pork, mixed with larger bits of pork fat and chiles, is used to produce this hard-dried salami. After being put into the skin, it is flattened, so the slices are rectangular.

MEAT 🐖

TYPE Dried

TYPICAL SIZE L: 16in (40cm), W: 2 x 5in (5 x 12cm)

ITALY Calabria

Zampone di Modena PGI

This is a delicacy made from ground pork meat, fat, and skin, sewn into the skin of a pig's trotter, then dried and cooked. Traditionally served hot with lentils to ring in a new year.

MEAT 🐖

TYPE Cooked

TYPICAL SIZE L: 7in (18cm), W: 2½in (6cm)

ITALY Modena, Emilia Romagna

65

SPAIN

Spanish sausages fall into two categories. The best known is chorizo, which is made everywhere and contains *pimentón* (Spanish paprika). However, in Catalonia most sausages are types of *butifarra*, which don't contain paprika. If a sausage name features the word *Ibérico* it is made of pork from the special Iberian black pig. Other words refer to shape and size, such as *vela* (stick), *ristra* (strings), *herradura* (hoop), or *rosario* (small and round).

Chorizo can be fresh, cured, or dried, smoked or unsmoked. The basic recipe is simply pork, salt, garlic, and paprika, but the permutations are endless. The paprika can be mild (sweet) or fiery, and is sometimes smoked; each region has its own particular flavor made from the local peppers. Another characteristic of many (but not all) chorizo is the tangy flavor imparted by the curing process, where the meat is fermented for a period before being stuffed into skins and then dried or smoked.

Botillo del Bierzo PGI

Giving its name to a tasty dish, this unusual pork sausage contains bones. Made with pieces of rib and tail, marinated in paprika, oregano, and garlic, it is smoked and dried. This sausage is usually cooked before eating.

MEAT 🐖

TYPE Cured

TYPICAL SIZE L: 8in (20cm), W: 5in (12cm)

SPAIN El Bierzo, Castile-León

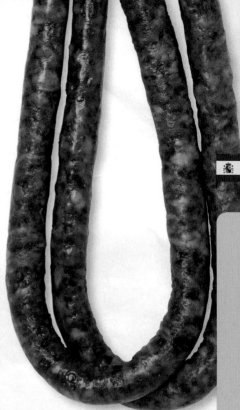

Bull blanc

A type of *butifarra*, this cooked Catalan white sausage is evenly marbled with lean and fat pork, tripe, and peppery spices. It is bound with bread crumbs, and stuffed into large skins. It is eaten cold with bread and tomatoes as a starter or in a salad.

MEAT

TYPE Cooked

TYPICAL SIZE L: 9in (23cm), W: 4in (10cm)

SPAIN Catalonia

Butifarra negra

Butifarra always contains pork, rind, offal, and seasonings, but no paprika. Its many variations include this blood sausage version, which can be used in cooked dishes or eaten cold without being cooked again. *Butifarra blanca* is a white sausage version.

MEAT

TYPE Cooked

TYPICAL SIZE L: 20in (50cm), W: 1½–2in (4–5cm)

SPAIN Catalonia

Chistorra

A very long and thin sausage made from pork and sometimes from beef, this has a red color that comes from a generous quantity of paprika. It can be either fresh or air dried, but is soft and is usually fried as a tapa.

MEAT and

TYPE Fresh or dried

TYPICAL SIZE L: 24in (60cm), W: ¾in (2cm)

SPAIN Navarre

Chorizo Asturiano

Lean and fat pork cuts are first oak-smoked, then cured in salt, sugar, oregano, garlic, and hot paprika, giving this sausage a punchy flavor. It is usually cooked with beans or is an ingredient in soups.

MEAT	
TYPE	Cured and dried
TYPICAL SIZE	L: 5in (12–13cm), W: 1in (3cm)
SPAIN	Asturias

Chorizo Cantimpalo

This colorful cured chorizo is a Segovian speciality. It is marbled with large chunks of cured fatty pork, and is flavored only with sea salt and smoked paprika. It is sliced thinly and eaten raw.

MEAT	
TYPE	Cured and dried
TYPICAL SIZE	L: 5½in (14cm), W: 2in (5cm)
SPAIN	Segovia, Castile-León

Chorizo de Pamplona

A thicker chorizo made with equal parts of finely chopped pork and beef and liberally spiced with paprika. It is cured and dried to get its classic deep orange color.

MEAT and	
TYPE	Cured and dried
TYPICAL SIZE	L: 16–18in (40–45cm), W: 3in (8cm)
SPAIN	Pamplona, Navarre

68

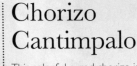

Chorizo de Salamanca

Chunks of loin and fat from the *Ibérico* pig are used to make this thick chorizo. After being marinated with salt, paprika, white wine, and olive oil, it is dry cured for 3 to 4 months.

MEAT 🐖

TYPE Cured and dried

TYPICAL SIZE L: 13in (33cm), W: 2in (5cm)

SPAIN Salamanca, Castile-León

Chorizo Gallego

Deep red and coarse-textured, this chorizo is flavored with oregano, garlic, and paprika. It is smoked before being cured, but has quite a mild flavor and is often fried, or baked in dishes, though it can also be eaten raw.

MEAT 🐖

TYPE Cured and dried

TYPICAL SIZE L: 5in (12cm), W: 1⅓in (4cm)

SPAIN Galicia

Chorizo Riojano PGI

This chorizo is made from pork loin and lard with garlic, and either mild or hot paprika from the Riojano pepper. It is the main ingredient of *patatas a la Riojana*.

MEAT 🐖

TYPE Cured and dried

TYPICAL SIZE L: 20in (50cm), W: 2in (5cm)

SPAIN La Rioja

69

Fuet

A slim dried sausage, known as *Espetec* in Barcelona. It is made from pork meat and cured lard with salt, ground white pepper, and a little sugar for sweetness. It is served freshly sliced with an apéritif.

MEAT

TYPE Cured and dried

TYPICAL SIZE
L: 13½in (35cm), W: 1in (3cm)

SPAIN Catalonia

Llonganissa de Pages

Longaniza is a long, thin, hard *butifarra* using pepper instead of paprika; it is popular all over Spain. Llonganissa de Pages is a dried Catalan version, eaten raw with bread.

MEAT

TYPE Cured and dried

TYPICAL SIZE
L: 13½in (35cm), W: 1in (3cm)

SPAIN Catalonia

Morcilla de Burgos

Morcilla (blood sausage), made from pig's blood, is popular all over Spain with additions as varied as beans, raisins, nuts, or squash. The famous Burgos variety contains rice, and is light, but well spiced.

MEAT

TYPE Cooked

TYPICAL SIZE L: 4in (10cm), W: 1½in (4cm)

SPAIN Burgos, Castile-León

Morcón Ibérico

Prepared from chunky, lean pork of expensive black Iberian pigs, fermented with garlic and paprika. Stuffed into a notably wide casing and tied into a bulbous shape, it is matured for at least 3 months. Sliced and eaten raw.

MEAT

TYPE Cured and dried

TYPICAL SIZE L: 8in (20cm), W: 4in (10cm)

SPAIN Andalusia and Extremadura

Salchichón de Vic PGI

This hard mountain sausage is made from pork with cracked black pepper, lightly smoked and then dried. Other versions of *salchichón* are popular all over Spain and may also be made with beef or venison.

MEAT

TYPE Dried

TYPICAL SIZE L: 12in (30cm), W: 1¼in (4cm)

SPAIN Plana de Vic, Catalonia

Sobrasada de Majorca

A dried but spreadable cured pork sausage, flavored with paprika and garlic. A red string means hot paprika, while a white string means mild. It is delicious eaten with fresh black figs.

MEAT

TYPE Cured

TYPICAL SIZE L: 16in (40cm), W: 2in (5cm)

SPAIN Mallorca

PORTUGAL

The traditional sausage-making areas of Portugal are those cool, mountainous regions where domestic wood fires would traditionally both smoke and dry the sausages to infuse flavor.

Many Portuguese sausages are not available outside their region and some are also seasonal, for example *chouriço de mel,* which is eaten as an autumnal dessert with honey poured over. Easily available throughout Portugal are the oval ceramic dishes called *assador* or *barca de chouriço,* specially made to flame and cook chouriço over pure alcohol at the table.

Sausages marked with "porco preto" are made from the black Alentejo pig whose diet of acorns gives its meat a superior flavor. Many of these products have been protected with PGI status. If marked "corrente," they are more industrial and formed into links instead of the very traditional loop. Portuguese sausages, like those of Spain, have been adopted by the countries they colonized. Versions of Portuguese chouriço and linguiça are found in Brazil and Goa, in India.

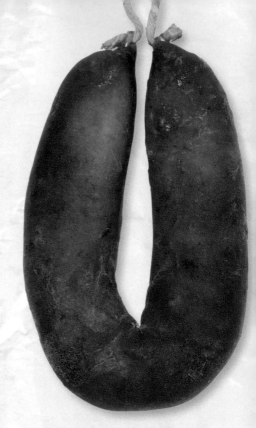

Alheira de Barroso-Montalegre PGI

Originally made by Jews from any white meat apart from pork, Alheira now often includes pork. This one is made from pork, chicken, and garlic, and is lightly smoked.

MEAT 🐖 and 🐓		
TYPE Cured		
TYPICAL SIZE L: 11in (28cm), W: 1½in (4cm)		
PORTUGAL Mirandela		

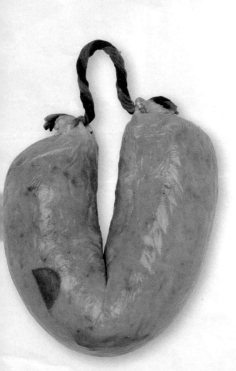

Alheira de caça

The deluxe version of Alheira is made from mixed game meats bound with bread crumbs and sometimes flavored with paprika and garlic. The sausage is cold smoked until golden.

MEAT 🦌 and 🦃

TYPE Fresh

TYPICAL SIZE L: 16in (40cm), W: 1½in (4cm)

PORTUGAL Central Portugal

Cacholeira preta

This black liver sausage is seasoned with both garlic and cumin and lightly smoked. Another soft, white version called *Cacholeira Branca* is made from pork fat, liver, kidney, and spleen.

MEAT 🐷

TYPE Cured and dried

TYPICAL SIZE L: 12in (30cm), W: 1½in (4cm)

PORTUGAL Alentejo

Chouriço de porco preto

Made from *porco preto*, the black Alentejo pig, this coarse-grained *chouriço* is of superior quality. It is oak smoked and dried, and can be eaten raw, or used in cooking.

MEAT 🐷

TYPE Cured and dried

TYPICAL SIZE L: 12in (30cm), W: 1in (3cm)

PORTUGAL Alentejo

73

Chouriço de sangue

A *chouriço* made from pig's blood. After cooking, it is smoked and dried to a rich black, then grilled or used in stews. There is also a white-skinned, poached Alentejo variety.

MEAT

TYPE Cooked

TYPICAL SIZE L: 16in (40cm), W: 1½in (4cm)

PORTUGAL Throughout, especially Alentejo

Chouriço de vinho

This sausage is made from high-quality pork. It is enriched with red wine and garlic before being smoked. A very rich *chouriço* with a deep brown color, it is usually shaped into rings or links.

MEAT

TYPE Cured and dried

TYPICAL SIZE L: 13in (34cm), W: 1in (3cm)

PORTUGAL Biera Alta

Chouriço mouro de Portalegre PGI

A black, smoked sausage made from finely ground Alentejo pork, heart, kidney, and fat. Garlic, sweet paprika, and sometimes Portalegre white wine or caraway seeds are also added.

MEAT

TYPE Cooked

TYPICAL SIZE L: 10in (25cm), W: 1in (3cm)

PORTUGAL Portalegre, Alto Alentejo

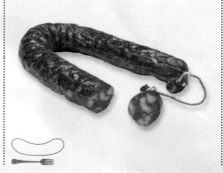

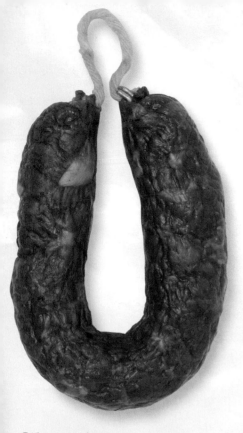

Chouriço Transmontano

This richly flavored sausage is from the mountains of northern Portugal. It is cured, then slowly smoked over holm oak in traditional smokehouses, to produce its distinctive flavor.

MEAT	
TYPE	Cured and dried
TYPICAL SIZE	L: 4in (10cm), W: 1in (2.5cm)
PORTUGAL	Trás-os-montana

Chouriço vermelho de colorau

As its name suggests, this sausage is colored red from the blood included with the meat. It is smoked and dried, though it remains quite soft. Delicious cooked with kale.

MEAT	
TYPE	Cured and dried
TYPICAL SIZE	L: 6in (15cm), W: 1in (3cm)
PORTUGAL	Throughout

Farinheira

A tangy white sausage made from wheat flour, cooked beef or pork fat, white wine, garlic, paprika, and occasionally orange juice. It is smoked for up to a week and has a soft texture. Farinheira must be cooked before being sliced.

MEAT	or
TYPE	Cooked
TYPICAL SIZE	L: 13½in (35cm), W: 1½in (4cm)
PORTUGAL	Throughout

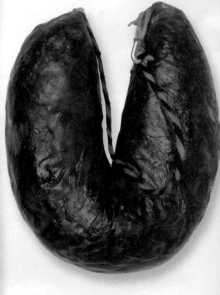

Linguiça

One of Portugal's most common sausages, linguiça is made from finely ground pork, garlic, paprika, oregano, and cumin. It is smoked and dried before being eaten, or more commonly added to stews.

Maranho

Also called *burlhões*, this sausage is made from the leg meat of goats reared in pine forests. Rice, ham, paprika, and especially mint, create its very distinctive flavor. It is cooked in the goat's stomach.

Morcela de arroz

This blood sausage is softened with cooked rice. *Morcela de arroz de Leiria* in Estremadura is renowned, and includes red wine, vinegar, and pork, with cumin, garlic, parsley, and cloves. They are eaten raw or cooked.

MEAT

TYPE Cured and dried

TYPICAL SIZE L: 12in (30cm), W: 1in (2.5cm)

PORTUGAL Throughout

MEAT

TYPE Cooked

TYPICAL SIZE L: 10in (25cm), W: 2½in (6cm)

PORTUGAL Beira Baixa

MEAT

TYPE Cooked

TYPICAL SIZE L: 6in (15cm), W: 2in (5cm)

PORTUGAL Throughout, especially Estremadura

76

Morcela tradicional

A well-spiced blood sausage made with pork fat and regional ingredients such as wine, flour, and cumin. *Moira* is another blood sausage variation. Eaten raw, or used in cooking.

MEAT

TYPE Cooked

TYPICAL SIZE L: 6in (15cm), W: 1¼in (3cm)

PORTUGAL Throughout

Paio

This is a thick, smoked sausage made with large pieces of pork loin. Along with garlic and paprika, the sausage has other flavors that depend on the region and include bay leaves, cumin, or wine.

MEAT

TYPE Cured and dried

TYPICAL SIZE L: 6in (15cm), W: 3in (7.5cm)

PORTUGAL Throughout, especially Alentejo

Salpicão

Large pieces of lean pork are marinated in wine, garlic, and paprika, then stuffed into a pig's stomach, before being smoked and dried. The Trás-os-montes salpicão are especially good.

MEAT

TYPE Dried

TYPICAL SIZE L: 10in (25cm), W: 3½in (9cm)

PORTUGAL Throughout, especially Trás-os-montes

77

UNITED KINGDOM AND REPUBLIC OF IRELAND

Affectionately known as "bangers," British and Irish sausages are distinctly different from those of other countries.

First of all, there is no tradition of making dried salami-style sausages; British sausages are either fresh, or they are cooked blood sausages. Second, there has always been a tradition of adding grains—originally bread crumbs—to the sausage mix, making British sausages both softer in texture and less rich than all-meat varieties, although all-meat sausages do exist. Most butchers use wheat-based twice-baked biscuits as the grains, and there are still artisan producers using natural grains like oatmeal and bread crumbs, or rice for gluten-free sausages.

English sausages are thick, with 6–8 of them weighing 1lb (450g). Scottish sausages are thinner, with 10–12 weighing 1lb (450g). The traditional British sausage is linked by hand into bunches; their length is determined by the width of the butcher's hand. Numerous kinds of international sausages are now available through delicatessens, butchers, and supermarkets.

Beef sausage

Deep pink, and with a strong, meaty flavor. Favorite additional flavorings to the standard beef sausage are horseradish or mustard. These are popular with Scots, who traditionally prefer beef to pork.

MEAT 🐄

TYPE Fresh

TYPICAL SIZE L: 4in (10cm), W: ¾in (2cm)

UK AND IRELAND Throughout, especially Scotland

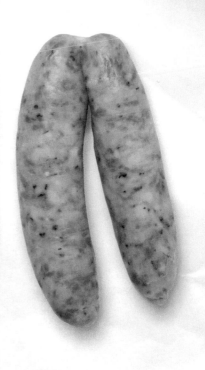

Black pudding
ENGLISH

Pork blood, onion, barley, and cubes of pork fat are the basic ingredients, with herbs more prevalent than spices. There are many variations. Lancashire's varieties use celery seed and pennyroyal (similar to spearmint).

MEAT		
TYPE	Cooked	
TYPICAL SIZE	L: 12in (30cm), W: 1½in (4cm)	
ENGLAND	Lancashire and the Black Country	

Black pudding
SCOTTISH

A smooth-textured pig's blood sausage with beef suet, oatmeal, and onion. Pepper is the predominant spice. Stornoway's famous black puddings were traditionally made from sheep or beef blood, as pigs were not common.

MEAT	and	
TYPE	Cooked	
TYPICAL SIZE	L: 20in (50cm), W: 3in (8cm)	
SCOTLAND	Throughout	

Chipolata

Short, slim sausages used for cocktail snacks and traditionally served wrapped in bacon during the holidays. These are largely made from pork, but other meats are occasionally used by artisan producers.

MEAT		
TYPE	Fresh	
TYPICAL SIZE	L: 3in (8cm), W: ¾in (2cm)	
UK AND IRELAND	Throughout	

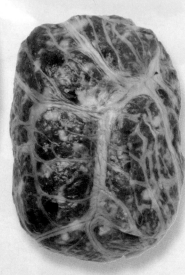

Cumberland sausage PGI

A popular coiled sausage, the Traditional PGI Cumberland sausage contains a minimum of 80 percent pork, chopped or minced coarsely. Typical flavorings include nutmeg, mace, cayenne, and black pepper.

MEAT 🐷

TYPE Fresh

TYPICAL SIZE
L: 39in (1 meter), W: 1in (3cm)

ENGLAND Cumbria

Faggot

A rich sausage made from minced pork belly, liver, heart, and sometimes lung, flavored with sage. The patties are wrapped in caul fat, baked, and served with onion gravy. They are named after the dialect word for a bundle of sticks, but are also known as "savory ducks."

MEAT 🐷

TYPE Fresh

TYPICAL SIZE L: 5in (12cm),
W: 2¼ x ¾in (7 x 2cm)

ENGLAND Black Country

Farmhouse sausage

A rustic style of sausage, the coarsely minced meat has more texture than traditional British sausages. They are usually made from pork but, these days, many artisan butchers make a farmhouse sausage using other meats and herbs.

MEAT 🐷

TYPE Fresh

TYPICAL SIZE L: 5in (12cm),
W: 1in (3cm)

UK AND IRELAND
Throughout

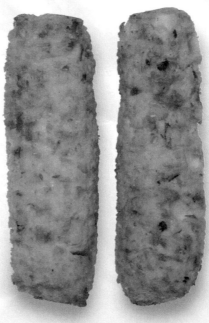

Game sausage

Game meats are usually lean, so pork fat is normally added to keep the sausage moist. Some are a mixture of game meats such as pheasant, venison, or wild boar. Parsley, thyme, and ginger are popular flavorings. Fresh game bird sausages are only available in season, which is in the autumn and winter.

MEAT 🐦 and 🦌

TYPE Fresh

TYPICAL SIZE L: 5in (12cm), W: 1in (3cm)

UK AND IRELAND Throughout

Glamorgan sausage

A hand-formed "sausage" made from Caerphilly cheese in place of meat. Mixed with leeks and bound with egg and bread crumbs or potato, they are formed into skinless "sausages" and fried to eat.

VEGETARIAN

TYPE Fresh

TYPICAL SIZE L: 8in (20cm), W: 1in (3cm)

WALES Glamorgan

Haggis

Sheep's heart, liver, and lungs, mixed with oatmeal and fat, then cooked to a crumbly texture. Ox casings are filled for small haggis, and a sheep's stomach for special occasions. It is often served with a shot of good single malt whisky.

MEAT 🐑

TYPE Cooked

TYPICAL SIZE L: 5in (12cm), W: 3½in (9cm)

SCOTLAND Throughout

Irish black pudding

Also known as Drisheen, this soft, fine-textured blood sausage is predominantly made from pig's blood, though the blood of other animals was traditionally also used, with bread crumbs, barley, and milk. It contains cream and is flavored with the herb tansy, which has notes similar to rosemary.

MEAT

TYPE Cooked

TYPICAL SIZE L: 7in (18cm)
W: 1¾in (4.5cm)

REPUBLIC OF IRELAND Co. Cork

Irish pork sausage

Ireland's pork is famous and her chunky pork sausages win countless awards. Flavorings include herbs such as marjoram and thyme. However, there are many inferior versions, so choose with care, visiting a good butcher and buying the best you can afford.

MEAT

TYPE Fresh

TYPICAL SIZE L: 4in (10cm),
W: 1in (3cm)

IRELAND Throughout Republic of Ireland and Northern Ireland

Jumbo sausage

Normally weighing about 3½oz (100g) each, these extra-long, thick sausages are popular at barbecues. They are generally made from pork, though other meats are occasionally used as well.

MEAT

TYPE Fresh

TYPICAL SIZE L: 8in (20cm),
W: 1½in (3.5cm)

UK AND IRELAND Throughout

Lamb sausage

Lamb sausages are less common than pork and beef, but are increasingly found at farmers' markets in sheep-rearing areas. Mint and rosemary are the most common flavorings used.

MEAT	
TYPE	Fresh
TYPICAL SIZE	L: 4in (10cm), W: ¾in (2cm)
UK AND IRELAND Throughout	

Lincolnshire sausage

Coarse-ground and chunky, these are less peppery in flavor than other British sausages. They are generally seasoned with a mixture of sage, nutmeg, ginger, and allspice.

MEAT	
TYPE	Fresh
TYPICAL SIZE	L: 5in (12cm), W: 1in (3cm)
ENGLAND Lincolnshire	

Lorne sausage

Also known as slicing sausage, this is a sausage made from pork, beef, or a mixture, formed into a brick and sliced into squares. Lorne sausage is a Scottish breakfast favorite, or is eaten in a roll. Its high fat content is one of its attractions.

MEAT and/or	
TYPE	Fresh
TYPICAL SIZE	L: 5in (12cm), W: 3 × ¾in (7.5 × 3cm)
SCOTLAND Glasgow	

British butchers maintain the tradition of linking their sausages by hand, but embrace international flavors, such as garlic and paprika.

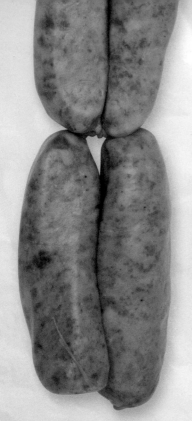

Newmarket sausage

Two Newmarket butchers both claim to make the authentic version. The main difference between the two pork sausages is texture: one uses twice-baked biscuits while the other adds bread crumbs.

MEAT

TYPE Fresh

TYPICAL SIZE L: 5in (12cm), W: 1in (3cm)

ENGLAND Newmarket

Oxford sausage

Veal sausages are not common in Britain nowadays; these sausages are an old, traditional recipe made from equal parts of pork and veal with added lemon juice, sage, thyme, and marjoram or savory. Originally skinless, the mixture is now stuffed into sausage skins.

MEAT and

TYPE Fresh

TYPICAL SIZE L: 5in (12cm), W: 1in (3cm)

ENGLAND Oxford

Pork and blood sausage

An increasingly popular sausage that combines two British favorites, the blood sausage lends a rich, sweet flavor to the minced pork. Apple is sometimes added to the mixture.

MEAT

TYPE Fresh

TYPICAL SIZE L: 5in (12cm), W: 1in (3cm)

UK AND IRELAND Throughout

Pork and leek sausage

Although considered a Welsh speciality, this is sold universally. It is an excellent combination, the sweetness of leeks contrasting well with the pork. Pork and apple, or cider, is another classic combination.

MEAT

TYPE Fresh

TYPICAL SIZE L: 5in (12cm), W: 1in (3cm)

UK AND IRELAND Throughout, especially Wales

Poultry sausage

Sold as a low-fat, healthy sausage, these are made with either chicken or turkey. They are usually spiced with flavors such as tarragon and cranberry and are popular in halal and kosher markets.

MEAT or

TYPE Fresh

TYPICAL SIZE L: 5in (12cm), W: 1in (3cm)

UK AND IRELAND Throughout

Saveloy

A red, smooth-textured, well-seasoned, smoked sausage, similar to a large hot dog. Now mainly industrially produced and with synthetic casings. Popular in fish and chip shops when battered and deep-fried.

MEAT

TYPE Cooked

TYPICAL SIZE L: 8in (20cm), W: 1in (3cm)

UK AND IRELAND Throughout

87

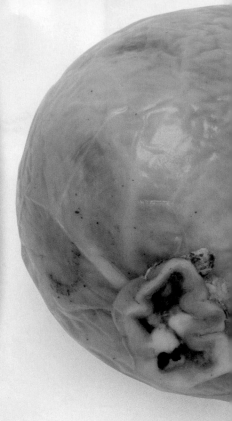

Steak sausage

A superior, slim sausage made from better-quality, leaner beef, and with a higher meat content (65–70 percent) than standard beef sausages. Usually sold as a Scottish butcher's speciality.

MEAT

TYPE Fresh

TYPICAL SIZE L: 5in (12cm), W: ¾in (2cm)

SCOTLAND Throughout

Vegetarian sausage

Vegetarian sausages replace meat with grains, beans, and sometimes tofu. They use a variety of herbs, spices, and oils, instead of meat fats. These always use synthetic casings.

VEGETARIAN

TYPE Fresh

TYPICAL SIZE L: 5in (12cm), W: 1in (3cm)

UK AND IRELAND Throughout

Venison haggis

The original haggis, this is made with deer liver, heart, lungs, suet, and oatmeal. Many recipes contain venison meat as well, which makes the haggis firm, dark, and rich.

MEAT

TYPE Cooked

TYPICAL SIZE L: 5in (12cm), W: 3½in (9cm)

SCOTLAND Highlands

Venison sausage

Venison is a dark, rich, tasty meat. Because it is also lean, the sausages often include pork fat in order to keep them moist. Typical spices used to flavor them include pepper, juniper, and ginger.

MEAT 🦌

TYPE Fresh

TYPICAL SIZE L: 5in (12cm), W: 1in (3cm)

UK AND IRELAND Throughout

White pudding

Called "mealie pudding" in Scotland, and "hog's pudding" in the English West Country, this is made from pork fat, oatmeal, onions, and suet. The English version also contains cooked pork.

MEAT 🐖

TYPE Cooked

TYPICAL SIZE L: 12in (30cm), W: 1½in (4cm)

UK AND IRELAND Throughout, especially Ireland and Scotland

Wild boar sausage

British boar are farmed, not wild, and they have enough fat, so there is no need to add any more. This is a rich, dark-fleshed sausage made with pork spices, sometimes juniper, as well as red wine.

MEAT 🐗

TYPE Fresh

TYPICAL SIZE L: 5in (12cm), W: 1in (3cm)

UK AND IRELAND Throughout

THE LOW COUNTRIES

This is another part of the world whose borders have shifted over the centuries and whose cuisines, and therefore sausages, reflect that fact. The southern, French-speaking part of Belgium makes sausages similar to those of northern France: a mixture of punchy dried *saucisson* and various delicious, well-flavored soft sausages: sweet black ones, green vegetable ones, grey tripe ones, and light, delicate white ones.

Farther north into Belgium's Flemish-speaking regions and up into Holland, the sausages become more like those of Germany, with cured and cooked sausages being the predominant type, along with a range of dried sausages. Holland's dried and fresh sausages were the basis of the boerewors of South Africa.

In both countries, there are sausages and soft sausages made especially for winter celebrations using seasonal vegetables. And in both countries, the Frankfurter type of sausage is very popular street food, eaten in Belgium with the ubiquitous fries and mayonnaise.

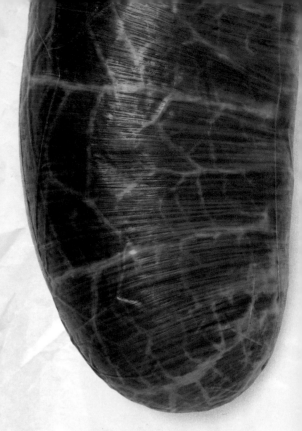

Bloedpens

Also called *bloempanch*, this Brussels speciality is a large blood sausage, but is unusual in being made with beef blood, and stuffed into beef guts. It is studded with pieces of pig's head meat, and spiced with cinnamon and nutmeg.

MEAT and

TYPE Cooked

TYPICAL SIZE L: 16in (40cm), W: 6in (15cm)

BELGIUM Brussels

Boterhammenworst

A large, mild sausage made from veal and pork fat. The meat is cured, and seasoned with ginger, pepper, nutmeg, and mace, and then it is lightly smoked and boiled. It should be eaten thinly sliced.

MEAT and

TYPE Cooked

TYPICAL SIZE L: 9½in (24cm), W: 3in (8cm)

HOLLAND Throughout

Boudin blanc de Liège

A famous speciality of Liège, this is a delicate white sausage made with finely minced, top-quality pork that is softened with egg, bread, milk, and onions. It is subtly flavored with marjoram.

MEAT

TYPE Cooked

TYPICAL SIZE L: 8in (20cm), W: 1½in (3.5cm)

BELGIUM Liège

Boudin noir à la flamande

A rich, slightly sweet blood sausage made from pig's blood, studded with cubes of pork fat, pieces of onion, and currants. It is flavored with cinnamon, cream, and brown sugar, and is usually served with applesauce.

MEAT

TYPE Cooked

TYPICAL SIZE L: 7in (18cm), W: 1in (3cm)

BELGIUM Wallonia

91

Braadworst

Also known as *saucijs*, this long, fresh pork sausage can be formed into a coil. It is grilled or fried, and is traditionally served with *stamppot* (crushed potatoes with vegetables), along with mayonnaise or mustard.

MEAT

TYPE Fresh

TYPICAL SIZE L: 5in (13cm), W: 1in (2.5cm)

BELGIUM AND HOLLAND Throughout

Droge worst

This is also called *metworst*, but is completely different from German Mettwurst. It is a coarsely minced and strongly flavored pork sausage, that comes from the windy, northern parts of Holland, where it is cured and then air dried.

MEAT

TYPE Cured and dried

TYPICAL SIZE L: 8½in (22cm), W: 1¾in (4.5cm)

HOLLAND Groningen, Friesland, and Drenthe

Gedroogde worst

A dried sausage, usually made from pork, with a white powdery skin formed during the drying process. Spicing varies from mild to spicy, while the Groningen version contains cloves. Sliced and eaten raw.

MEAT

TYPE Dried

TYPICAL SIZE L: 7in (18cm), W: 1½in (4cm)

HOLLAND Throughout

Gelderse rookworst

A smoked, cooked sausage from Gelderland which was renowned for its particularly fine pork. Inferior rookworst has only smoke flavoring, but better-quality examples are smoked. They are traditionally eaten with kale.

MEAT

TYPE Cooked

TYPICAL SIZE L: 5in (12cm), W: 1in (2.5cm)

HOLLAND Throughout, especially Gelderland

Ossenworste

Not unlike steak tartare, this cured sausage is eaten raw. It is made from ground beef, flavored with pepper, cloves, mace, and nutmeg. Some versions are slowly smoked at a low temperature, but remain raw.

MEAT

TYPE Cured

TYPICAL SIZE L: 5in (12cm), W: 2in (5cm)

HOLLAND Amsterdam

Saucisson d'Ardennes

From the famous ham-making region, this is a finely minced pork sausage with juniper, that is cured and then heavily smoked over oak and beechwood, before being dried. Each of the many sizes has a different name.

MEAT

TYPE Cured and dried

TYPICAL SIZE L: 6½in (17cm), W: 1½in (4cm)

BELGIUM The Ardennes

93

SCANDINAVIA

Scandinavian cooking reflects its northern climate where long winters made it necessary to preserve meat and fish. As well as salting and smoking their food, Scandinavians use sugar to keep the meat soft, and this salty-sweet taste is a characteristic found in many Scandinavian sausages.

In the north, lamb, mutton, and venison, are the staple meats, and sometimes, horse meat or even bear meat can appear on the menu or in cured products. In Denmark, pork and beef are most commonly used to make sausages.

Some sausage names are similar in neighboring countries, but it helps to know the basic words. The Norwegian and Danish word for sausage is *pølse*; in Sweden it is *korv*; in Finland, *makkara* or *vursti*; and in Iceland, *pylsa*. Southern Scandinavian sausages veer toward German styles; in the far north they become more like Polish kiełbasa. In between is a rich and interesting feast of unusual sausages.

Algkorv

Venison sausages are typical of Norway and Sweden, both from elk and reindeer (renkorv), which in Norway are called *Reinsdyrpølse*. They can be cured or dried, and flavorings include juniper or cloves, cinnamon, and ginger. Swedes eat more venison than anyone else in the world.

MEAT 🦌 and 🦌

TYPE Cured or dried

TYPICAL SIZE L: 12½in (32cm), W: 1½in (4cm)

SWEDEN AND NORWAY Throughout

Falukorv TSG

Made from a mixture of beef or veal and pork, this hot-smoked sausage must contain more than 40 percent meat and be bound with potato starch to be called Falukorv. It is cooked, and either fried, simmered, or used in recipes. Also known as "Lyoner" sausage. It was brought to Sweden by German miners.

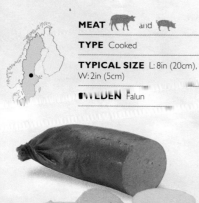

MEAT and

TYPE Cooked

TYPICAL SIZE L: 8in (20cm), W: 2in (5cm)

SWEDEN Falun

Isterband

There are many variations of this coarsely minced, smoked pork sausage, but its characteristic sour flavor comes from being cured. The other ingredients are whole barley and sometimes mashed potato. It can be dried or left undried.

MEAT

TYPE Cured, or cured and dried

TYPICAL SIZE L: 9½in (24cm), W: 1½in (3.5cm)

SWEDEN Throughout, especially Småland

Kødpølse

A cold-cutting sausage made from finely ground lean pork, lard, and onions, then stuffed into wide casings and cooked. It is sliced and eaten as a popular breakfast item, or as part of a mixture of cold cuts.

MEAT

TYPE Cooked

TYPICAL SIZE L: 12in (30cm), W: 2¾in (7cm)

DENMARK Throughout

Leverkorv

Swedish liver sausage is made with pork liver and sometimes veal, with milk, mashed potato, onion, white pepper, and marjoram. It is pounded to a fine paste, put into skins, and simmered, but it is not usually smoked.

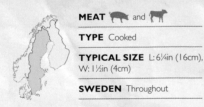

MEAT 🐷 and 🐄

TYPE Cooked

TYPICAL SIZE L: 6¼in (16cm), W: 1½in (4cm)

SWEDEN Throughout

Leverpølse

This fairly soft, liver sausage is made from lean pork meat, pork liver, and fat, flavored with allspice, pepper, onions, and sometimes cardamom. It is cooked and then heavily smoked, and served cold on bread. Similar is *leverpostej*, a more spreadable version flavored with anchovies.

MEAT 🐷

TYPE Cooked

TYPICAL SIZE L: 11in (28cm), W: 2¾in (7cm)

DENMARK Throughout

Medister pølse

Sometimes just called *Medister*, this long, pale sausage is made from finely minced pork meat and back fat, flavored with onions, allspice, and cloves. It is rolled up into a spiral, and lengths are cut off for frying or grilling.

MEAT 🐷

TYPE Fresh

TYPICAL SIZE L: 18in (45cm), W: 1in (3cm)

DENMARK AND NORWAY Throughout

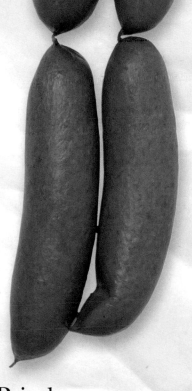

Morrpølse

There are many different recipes for this sausage. It can be made from venison, pork, or heart, and can include the blood. Flavorings include ginger or juniper, and typically, syrup. It is normally a dried sausage, but can also be fresh. Similar is *Fårepøls*, made from mutton and pork.

MEAT and

TYPE Fresh or dried

TYPICAL SIZE L: 8in (20cm), W: 1½in (4cm)

NORWAY Throughout

Mustamakkara

A slim, blood sausage made particularly dark by the addition of rye flour. Whole grains of barley or rye are included, which give an interesting texture. It is served hot with lingonberry jam, and is popular street food at the market in Tampere. Milk is the traditional drink to have with mustamakkara.

MEAT

TYPE Cooked

TYPICAL SIZE L: 9in (23cm), W: 1in (2.5cm)

FINLAND Tampere, Pirkanmaa

Prinskorv

These are short, linked versions of Frankfurter sausage, though they are usually fried rather than boiled. Because of their small size, they are called "Prince" sausages, and they are a popular feature of the Swedish Christmas *smörgåsbord*. Also enjoyed as a cold snack on a picnic.

MEAT

TYPE Cooked

TYPICAL SIZE L: 3in (8cm), W: ¾in (2cm)

SWEDEN Throughout

97

alle tiders smag

3-STJERNET

- alle tiders smag

3-STJERNET

Rød pølse

Greatly enjoyed as street food, this "red sausage" is an unsmoked, hot-dog style of sausage, whose main characteristic is its skin, which is colored bright red with carmine. Dill pickles, fried onions, and mustard are the favorite accompaniments.

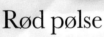

MEAT 🐷

TYPE Cooked

TYPICAL SIZE L: 8in (20cm), W: ¾in (2cm)

DENMARK AND NORWAY Throughout

Ryynimakkara

Made with a high percentage of cooked *ryyni* (oat or barley groats) flavored with ginger, cloves, and pepper, this sausage originally contained no meat, though nowadays it does. Pork makes a pale sausage; lamb or beef make it darker. It is usually fried. *Perunamakkara* is rather similar, but uses potato instead of barley.

MEAT 🐷 or 🐑

TYPE Fresh

TYPICAL SIZE L: 6in (15cm), W: 1in (3cm)

FINLAND Throughout

Salami

A mixture of medium-grained meats such as pork, beef, or veal are flavored with garlic and coriander, and sometimes also wine and paprika. It is typically a bright pink color and often appears at the breakfast table. Superior versions are sugar-glazed before being dried.

MEAT 🐷 and 🐷

TYPE Cured and dried

TYPICAL SIZE L: 16in (40cm), W: 3½in (9cm)

DENMARK Throughout

Spegepølse

Spegepølse is the most common type of Danish sausage, and many forms exist. Pork is the most usual filling but beef, lamb, venison, and even vegetables such as cabbage or potatoes may be added. The sausages are cured, smoked, and dried.

MEAT and

TYPE Cured and dried

TYPICAL SIZE L: 10in (25cm), W: 2½in (6cm)

DENMARK Throughout

Spekepølse

This is the name of a family of cured and dried sausages, the fermentation process giving them their typical tangy flavor. They can be made from almost any kind of meat (most commonly pork or mutton), but should not have more than 27 percent fat. They can also be smoked.

MEAT or

TYPE Cured and dried

TYPICAL SIZE L: 8½in (21cm), W: 2in (5cm)

NORWAY Throughout

Vildsvinsalami

This wild boar salami is made from one of the two most popular wild meats in Sweden, venison being the other one. Both are dark, lean meats with an intense flavor, and they are often flavored with juniper and garlic.

MEAT

TYPE Dried

TYPICAL SIZE L: 8in (20cm), W: 1¾in (4.5cm)

SWEDEN Throughout

99

POLAND

Polish cuisine is a mixture of hearty Slavic cooking with Italian and French influences dating back to medieval times. Nowadays, Poles will say their two most important foods are bread and sausages, and the wealth of examples confirms this, as do famous dishes such as *bigos*—a cabbage stew that is packed with different meats and sausages.

"Kiełbasa" means simply "sausage," and people often drop this word from the name. They play their part as celebration food; for example, many of the white sausages are popular at Easter.

During Poland's 50 years of Communist rule, traditional foods were standardized. This strict regulation meant that, although they lost some of their original character, the high quality of each sausage was maintained throughout the country, and Polish sausages enjoyed an excellent reputation.

Another result of standardization is that, although many kiełbasa originated in, and are named after, towns and regions, the sausages are in reality made all over Poland. Sausages—many of which are fermented—are also named after their characteristic ingredients, such as lemon, bacon, garlic, or juniper.

Baleron

Large pieces of pork collar are pressed into a skin, the marbled fat content keeping it moist as it is smoked and cooked. Usually served cold, the sausage is sometimes also fried.

MEAT 🐗

TYPE Cooked

TYPICAL SIZE L: 12in (30cm), W: 5in (12cm)

POLAND Throughout

Blok Ozorkowy

This huge blood sausage, made from pig's blood, is speckled with small pieces of fat packed around large chunks of pickled tongue and pork. It is eaten both hot and cold, and the thick skin is usually removed.

MEAT

TYPE Cooked

TYPICAL SIZE L: 14in (36cm), W: 5in (13cm)

POLAND Throughout, especially Ozorków

Kabanos

A finger-thin hunter's sausage made from lean pork, seasoned with pepper, juniper, garlic, caraway, and allspice, then smoked and dried. Popular everyday snacks, they are also used for celebrations.

MEAT

TYPE Cured and dried

TYPICAL SIZE L: 12in (30cm), W: ½in (1cm)

POLAND Throughout

Kaszanka

A pig's blood sausage made with minced liver, lungs, and fat, as well as onion and marjoram. Buckwheat or barley groats give it a crumbly texture. Kaszanka is simmered or fried.

MEAT

TYPE Cooked

TYPICAL SIZE L: 4in (10cm), W: 1½in (4cm)

POLAND Throughout

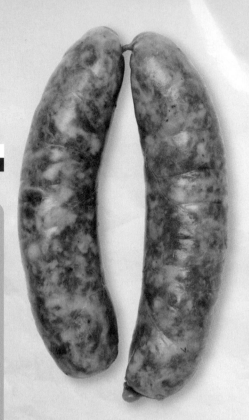

Kiełbasa biała

A fresh, white sausage made from pork and veal, or beef, flavored with pepper, garlic, and marjoram. It can be eaten with sauerkraut and potatoes, or used in soups, especially at Easter.

 MEAT 🐷 and 🐄

TYPE Fresh

TYPICAL SIZE L: 5in (12cm), W: 1½in (3.5cm)

POLAND Throughout

Kiełbasa czosnkowa

A long sausage made from cured pork, with pepper and marjoram. The characteristic flavor comes from a strong measure of fresh garlic. It is simmered, then lightly smoked.

 MEAT 🐷

TYPE Cooked

TYPICAL SIZE L: 10in (25cm), W: 1in (3cm)

POLAND Throughout

Kiełbasa Lisiecka PGI

Coarsely chopped chunks of very lean pork are flavored with pepper and garlic, then looped on to sticks, and hot smoked and dried over hardwood. This is quite a salty sausage.

 MEAT 🐷

TYPE Cured and dried

TYPICAL SIZE L: 9in (23cm), W: 1½in (3.5cm)

POLAND Throughout, especially Krakow and Liszki

Kiełbasa myśliwska

A coarse-cut hunter's sausage made from pork (and sometimes beef as well), with pepper, sugar, and juniper. Hot-smoked twice over beech to a deep brown, it is eaten on rye bread.

MEAT and

TYPE Cured and dried

TYPICAL SIZE L: 6in (15cm), W: 1½in (3.5cm)

POLAND Throughout

Kiełbasa podwawelska

A high-quality, nicely marbled pork and garlic sausage that is made into long, slim loops, then lightly smoked and roasted. Cheaper versions contain poultry. It is served cold, or grilled.

MEAT

TYPE Cured and dried

TYPICAL SIZE L: 18in (45cm), W: 1in (3cm)

POLAND Throughout, especially Wawel, Krakow

Kiełbasa Toruńska

Originally from the medieval town of Toruń, this is a slim sausage, normally made from pork but sometimes chicken too. The traditional long loops—which are draped over sticks to be dried—are hot smoked.

MEAT and

TYPE Cured and dried

TYPICAL SIZE L: 10in (25cm), W: ¾in (2cm)

POLAND Throughout, especially Toruń, Kujawy-Pomerania Province

103

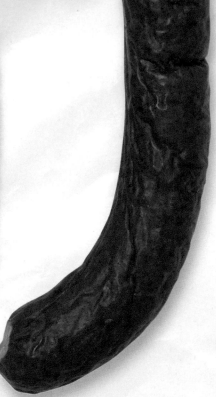

Kiełbasa wiejska

A fine-textured, country-style sausage made from pork and veal, flavored with pepper, marjoram, and garlic. It is scalded in hot water and then hot smoked, usually in long loops, though it can come in other shapes.

MEAT 🐷 and 🐄

TYPE Cooked

TYPICAL SIZE L: 8in (20cm), W: 1in (3cm)

POLAND Throughout

Kiełbasa zwyczajna

A mountain sausage made from cured pork and beef, with pepper, fresh garlic, and sometimes marjoram. It is heavily smoked before being cut into pieces and used for soup and stews.

MEAT 🐷 and 🐄

TYPE Cured and dried

TYPICAL SIZE L: 9in (23cm), W: 1½in (3.5cm)

POLAND Throughout, especially Zyweic

Krakowska

A chunky sausage marbled with pieces of lean pork, and flavored with allspice, coriander, and garlic. It is cooked and hot smoked, so eaten cold. *Krakowska sucha* is a dried version.

MEAT 🐷

TYPE Cooked

TYPICAL SIZE L: 12in (30cm), W: 3in (8cm)

POLAND Throughout, especially Krakow

Parówka

A stubby, Frankfurter-style sausage made from finely ground pork or beef, with chicken often used to extend the more expensive meats; some include cheese. They are linked and briefly boiled, and are popularly served—recooked—for breakfast.

MEAT	
TYPE	Cooked
TYPICAL SIZE	L: 5in (12cm), W: ¾in (2cm)
POLAND	Throughout

Pasztetowa

Sometimes called *kiszka pasztetowa*, this popular pork and liver spreading sausage is flavored with marjoram. Another version of the sausage includes semolina. It is sometimes lightly smoked.

MEAT	
TYPE	Cooked
TYPICAL SIZE	L: 10in (25cm), W: 2in (5cm)
POLAND	Throughout

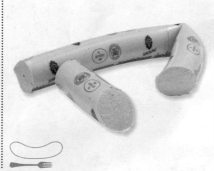

Salceson

Poland's version of headcheese, that is sliced and eaten cold. There are many variations: *salceson czarny* contains blood, *salceson Ozorkowy* includes tongue, while others have offal, liver, and different spices.

MEAT	
TYPE	Cooked
TYPICAL SIZE	L: 6in (15cm), W: 4in (10cm)
POLAND	Throughout

Kiełbasa wiejska, or "country sausage," is a favorite for its garlicky, smoked flavor and is found in various forms throughout Poland.

Many Polish sausages are smoked, giving them a deep color. The white bloom on the skin indicates a prolonged drying period.

CENTRAL AND EASTERN EUROPE AND RUSSIA

The countries in this section were once part of the former Soviet Bloc, and their sausages became standardized. During the Second World War, Russia's meat industry was destroyed and vast factories were set up to feed a nation hungry for sausages. The quality was often so poor that they were the butt of many jokes, and people would travel into Moscow on the "sausage train" to try to buy sausages that were worth eating. It is telling that the Soviet dream consisted of sausages and freedom.

The result of decades of centralized food production was that the number of varieties of sausages being made was only around 200 —a small number for such a large area. But although a great many of them still conform to the Soviet type, the countries of the former Soviet Union have begun to resurrect their own regional sausages, with several earning PGI status in the last decade.

Csabai kolbász PGI

This deep, fiery red *kolbász* is a popular salami sausage, speckled with pieces of fat. Colored and flavored with hot paprika, it is then smoked. There are several shapes and sizes.

MEAT 🐖

TYPE Cured and dried

TYPICAL SIZE L: 7in (18cm), W: ¾in (2cm)

HUNGARY Throughout, especially Békéscsaba

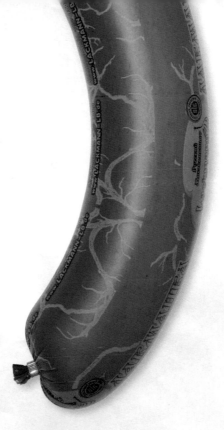

Debreceni kolbász

A fine-textured scalded sausage, heavily spiced with paprika, garlic, pepper, and marjoram, which can be unsmoked or lightly smoked. It is eaten baked or grilled, and served with *lesco*: a deliciously contrasting relish made from sweet peppers.

MEAT 🐷

TYPE Cooked

TYPICAL SIZE L: 7in (18cm), W: 1in (3cm)

HUNGARY Throughout, especially Debrecen

Doctorskaya

Designed by Soviet doctors, this is a nutritious, smooth, creamy sausage. Made from beef, pork, eggs, and milk, flavored with nutmeg and cardamom, the original version is unsmoked, though smoked versions also exist. It is sliced and eaten cold.

MEAT 🐮 and 🐷

TYPE Cooked

TYPICAL SIZE L: 10in (26cm), W: 2½in (6cm)

RUSSIA Throughout

Gruzinskaya

A cold-smoked dried sausage made with beef and sometimes pork as well, flavored with sugar, brandy, and typical Caucasian spices such as fenugreek, coriander, turmeric, dill, and basil.

MEAT 🐮 and 🐷

TYPE Cured and dried

TYPICAL SIZE L: 10in (25cm), W: 1½in (4cm)

RUSSIA Throughout, especially Caucasus

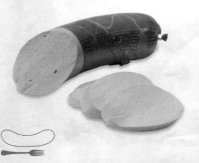

Jitrnice

A popular cooked sausage made from pig's head meat and skin mixed with liver, heart, tongue, and barley groats, flavored with garlic and pepper. *Jelítko* is similar, made from pig's blood studded with pieces of pork, spiced with garlic, ginger, allspice, and marjoram. Traditionally they were closed at each end with wooden twigs.

MEAT

TYPE Cooked

TYPICAL SIZE L: 7in (18cm), W: 1½in (4cm)

CZECH REPUBLIC Throughout

Karlovska lukanka PGI

A spicy pork and beef salami flavored with cumin and fenugreek. It has a flattened oval shape. Those with natural casings have a white mold on the skin. *Smedovska lukanka* is smoked and is made with caraway.

MEAT and

TYPE Dried

TYPICAL SIZE L: 8½in (22cm), W: 1 x 2in (3 x 5cm)

BULGARIA Throughout, especially Karlovo and Smyadovo

Kindziukas

This was traditionally a bulbous sausage made from a pig's stomach stuffed with coarsely chopped pork, garlic, and pepper. It was slowly dried under the roof and acquired a smoky flavor from the wood fire. Nowadays, a cylindrical form is more usual.

MEAT

TYPE Cured and dried

TYPICAL SIZE L: 10in (26cm), W: 2¾in (7cm)

LITHUANIA Throughout, especially Aukštaitija

110

Klobása čorizo

The Czech word *klobása* can refer to many types of sausage. On its own it often refers to a thick hot dog-style sausage containing high-quality meat. This one is a cured chorizo-style of sausage flavored with paprika, and smoked to a deep, rich brown.

MEAT 🐖

TYPE Cured and dried

TYPICAL SIZE L: 7in (18cm), W: 1in (3cm)

CZECH REPUBLIC Throughout

Kolbasa

Kolbasa comes from *kiełbasa* (Polish sausages) which were much sought-after in Soviet Russia, and the word covers any sausage that is not a fresh one, from dried to cured, from smoked to cooked. This one is a smooth, cooked sausage for slicing.

MEAT 🐖

TYPE Cured, cooked, or dried

TYPICAL SIZE L: 8in (20cm), W: 2½in (6cm)

RUSSIA Throughout

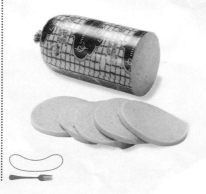

Kracowskaya

A high-grade pork sausage that is well marbled with large chunks of lean pork, and flavored with pepper, garlic, and coriander. It is cooked and smoked, and usually served cold. Named after Krakow in Poland, whose sausages are highly regarded.

MEAT 🐖

TYPE Cured

TYPICAL SIZE L: 10in (25cm), W: 2in (5cm)

RUSSIA Throughout

Kulenova seka

This is a small version of *kulen*, which is
a large sausage made in the pig's stomach,
that is smoked and then dried for up to
a year. Hot paprika gives a fiery taste and
an orange-red color.

MEAT 🐖

TYPE Dried

TYPICAL SIZE L: 6¼in (16cm),
W: 2in (5cm)

CROATIA AND SERBIA
Throughout

Lovecký salám

One of the many types of Czech salami,
this one is a hunter's sausage, flattened
between boards into an oblong section.
It is dry and a bright color, speckled with
medium-ground pieces of fat.

MEAT 🐖

TYPE Cured and dried

TYPICAL SIZE L: 16in (40cm),
W: 2 × ½in (5 × 1cm)

CZECH REPUBLIC
Throughout

Mangalica

Made from the meat of the curly-coated
fat Mangalica pig, this long sausage is bright
orange from sweet paprika. Cold-smoked
and dried for 3 months, it is eaten with
pickled vegetables.

MEAT 🐖

TYPE Cured and dried

TYPICAL SIZE L: 6in (15cm),
W: 1in (3cm)

HUNGARY Kiskunság

Mititei

Small, skinless sausages formed into lengths, then chilled and charcoal grilled. Made from lamb, pork, beef, or a mixture, they are flavored with hot paprika, dill, caraway, and garlic. Typically served with mustard and beer.

MEAT 🐑 and/or 🐖

TYPE Fresh

TYPICAL SIZE L: 3½in (9cm), W: 1in (3cm)

ROMANIA Throughout

Moskovskaya

Also called *Moskovskaya kolbasa*, this robust salami is made from coarsely minced pork and beef, liberally studded with chunks of lard. It is strongly flavored with garlic, and is given a lengthy smoking time.

MEAT 🐖 and 🐄

TYPE Cured and dried

TYPICAL SIZE L: 10in (25cm), W: 1½in (4cm)

RUSSIA Throughout, especially Moscow

Poltavskaya

Ukraine is famed for its excellent sausages. This one is made from pork and beef with a high proportion of fat, evenly spread throughout the slice. It is lightly hot smoked, which cooks it, and eaten raw.

MEAT 🐖 and 🐄

TYPE Cooked

TYPICAL SIZE L: 10in (26cm), W: 2in (5cm)

RUSSIA AND UKRAINE Throughout

113

Pressburg salama

Pressburg is German for Bratislava where, during the Austro-Hungarian Empire, the smokehouses had a special license to make sausages for the Emperor. This is a long-lasting, hot-smoked sausage that is sliced and served cold.

MEAT

TYPE Cured

TYPICAL SIZE L: 12in (30cm), W: 2¾in (7cm)

SLOVAKIA Throughout, especially Bratislava

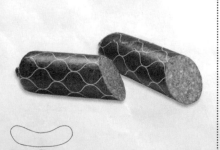

Skilandinė

A wrinkled pork and beef sausage with large cubes of back fat. Its spiciness comes from mustard seed and garlic, and it is cured, cold smoked, and dried. This cylindrical version is similar to the traditional bulbous or drop-shaped *Skilandis*.

MEAT and

TYPE Cured and dried

TYPICAL SIZE L: 13in (33cm), W: 1½in (4cm)

LITHUANIA Throughout

Sosiska

A generic Russian term for fresh scalded sausages. They are usually made from beef, pork, and lard, with some milk to moisten them. They are lightly smoked. *Sardelki* have coarser-grained meat and are thicker and shorter.

MEAT and

TYPE Cooked

TYPICAL SIZE L: 6in (15cm), W: 1in (3cm)

RUSSIA Throughout

Špekáčky

A short, stubby Frankfurter sausage, containing a high proportion of bacon fat, these are popularly cooked over the camp fire. When pickled in vinegar in glass jars, they are called *Utopenci* (drowned men).

MEAT

TYPE Cooked

TYPICAL SIZE L: 4½in (11cm), W: 1½in (4cm)

CZECH REPUBLIC Throughout

Téliszalámi

A smoked and slowly air-dried "winter salami" flavored with white pepper and allspice. *Szegedi téliszalámi* and *Budapesti téliszalámi* are made from the meat of Mangalica pigs; both have PGI status.

MEAT

TYPE Dried

TYPICAL SIZE L: 20in (50cm), W: 2in (5cm)

HUNGARY Throughout, especially Budapest and Szeged

Tokajská saláma

This Slovak sausage is actually Hungarian in origin. It is a cured and dried salami, made from pork and beef, with whole white peppercorns, cumin, and a high proportion of paprika, which gives its typically Hungarian color and flavor.

MEAT and

TYPE Cured and dried

TYPICAL SIZE L: 12in (30cm), W: 2in (5cm)

HUNGARY AND SLOVAKIA Throughout

EASTERN MEDITERRANEAN

The countries around the Eastern Mediterranean are renowned for their delicious and delicately spiced little parcels of meat. Sometimes, the line between what constitutes a sausage and simply minced meat—perhaps wrapped in a vine leaf—is a little blurred, but the common element is their light spicing and the flavor imparted by being cooked on charcoal grills. Unlike the sausages of northern and Alpine Europe, most of the sausages from around the Eastern Mediterranean tend to be freshly made and cooked at once. There is still a strong tradition of making sausages in many country areas.

Sausages often appear as part of a *meze*: that tempting array of small dishes that appears at lunchtime or before a substantial meal. They are accompanied by a mixture of such things as tiny balls of fresh cheese, some olives, yogurt and cucumber, some fried seafood, or an eggplant salad.

Horiatiko

A spicy *loukaniko* (sausage), usually made from pork. They are flavored with red and black pepper, cumin, and sometimes orange peel. There are two types: one powerfully flavored with oregano, and the other, from Thessaly, made with copious quantities of leeks.

MEAT 🐖	
TYPE Fresh	
TYPICAL SIZE L: 4in (10cm), W: 1in (3cm)	
GREECE Throughout, especially Thessaly	

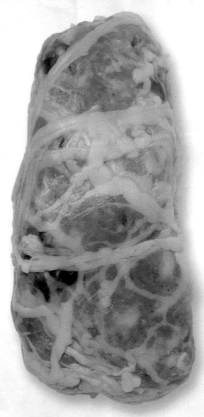

Makanek

A meaty, fresh sausage made from lamb and beef (or pork), these sausages sometimes have pine nuts in them. The spicing will include cumin. They are fried and served with pomegranate syrup drizzled over them.

MEAT 🐑 and 🐖

TYPE Fresh

TYPICAL SIZE L: 4in (10cm)
W: 1in (3cm)

LEBANON Throughout

Sheftalia

Made from lamb or pork with onions, parsley, and cinnamon, sheftalia are wrapped in caul fat instead of being stuffed into skins. They are threaded on skewers, grilled, and served sprinkled with lemon juice in pita bread.

MEAT 🐑 or 🐖

TYPE Fresh

TYPICAL SIZE L: 4in (10cm),
W: 2in (5cm)

CYPRUS Throughout

Soudjouk

Also known as *sujuk*, *sukuk*, or *sucuk*, this mahogany-red, dry sausage is ubiquitous throughout the region. Usually made from beef, though pork can be used, it is spiced with garlic, fenugreek, allspice, cumin, sumac, and paprika. It is eaten both raw and cooked.

MEAT 🐖 or 🐑

TYPE Part-dried or dried

TYPICAL SIZE L: 5in (13cm),
W: 1in (3cm)

LEBANON, TURKEY, AND SYRIA Throughout

NORTH AFRICA

The cuisine of **North Africa** is more akin to that of the **Middle East** and **Mediterranean** fringes than that of the rest of **Africa**. Spices, though not necessarily hot, are often highly complex mixtures containing romantic-sounding ingredients such as dried rosebuds, fenugreek, or sumac. Although these pastes and seasonings may have generic names such as *harīsa*, *bahārāt*, or *tābil*, there are countless family recipes, all of which are different.

Lamb and goat are the most common animals used for sausages in this region, though veal is a popular alternative, and offal is highly prized. Pork sausages are less common here due to the prevalence of Islam. As in nearby regions, many minced meat preparations are not stuffed into sausage skins. Like the dried meat preparations *khlea* (highly seasoned mutton and offal preserved in hot fat), and *qadīd* (spiced mutton or goat preserved in oil), dried *mirqāz* are also sometimes cooked and preserved in olive oil.

Merguez

Morocco's version of *mirqāz* is this spicy red sausage, usually made from lamb or beef, but occasionally pork, reflecting the time when Morocco was a French colony. It is flavored with paprika. Versions of this sausage appear in many other countries.

MEAT 🐑 or 🐄	
TYPE Fresh	
TYPICAL SIZE L: 5in (13cm), W: ¾in (2cm)	
MOROCCO Throughout	

Mirqāz

This sausage has many spellings, and appears throughout North Africa. Normally made from lamb or goat, there are also veal or offal versions, and it can be fresh or air dried. Flavorings include preserved lemons, *harīsa*, and hot chiles, which make it red.

MEAT 🐑 or 🐐

TYPE Fresh or dried

TYPICAL SIZE L: 3½in (9cm), W: 1in (3cm)

ALGERIA AND TUNISIA Throughout

Saucisse Marocaine

These fresh or lightly cured lamb or beef sausages are usually seasoned with *harīsa*, the typical spice mix of the region, which is a complex blend of fragrant and piquant spices. There is also a dried version called *mjebna*.

MEAT 🐑 or 🐄

TYPE Fresh or cured

TYPICAL SIZE L: 5in (13cm), W: ¾in (2cm)

MOROCCO Throughout

Sujuk

This red beef sausage has a milder flavor than Eastern Mediterranean versions, but typical spices are paprika, sumac, allspice, garlic, cumin, and fenugreek. It comes fresh or dried, and is both fried and used in dishes.

MEAT 🐄

TYPE Fresh or dried

TYPICAL SIZE L: 3in (8cm), W: 1in (3cm)

EGYPT Throughout

119

SOUTH AFRICA

The word *boerewors* epitomizes South African food, conjuring up a picture of conviviality around the traditional *braai*— the grill on which these coils of sausages are cooked. When not coiled, a generous link is perfect for the popular "boerie roll."

Dutch settlers of the seventeenth century were responsible for this famous sausage; its name evolved from the words *boer* (farmer) and *worst* (sausage). There are dozens of different kinds, with spices ranging from comparatively simple mixes to fiery African flavors. The hot climate has made South Africa famous for its biltong (dried lean meat) and dried sausages, and spices play a dual role in these, to both flavor the meat and to deter flies. Apart from nutmeg and cloves, coriander seed is widely used.

South African sausages are not usually cured; they are eaten fresh or quickly dried. But most recipes include a splash of vinegar, which helps to preserve them, and gives them their characteristic and much-loved flavor.

Boerewors

A fresh, coarsely minced sausage usually made from beef (though many other meats can be used) and usually formed into a coil for grilling. Typical flavorings include nutmeg, cloves, coriander, allspice, and vinegar. They are often served with a maize-meal porridge.

MEAT

TYPE Fresh

TYPICAL SIZE L: 24–32in (60–80cm), W: 1in (3cm)

SOUTH AFRICA Throughout

Chakalaka boerewors

Made from any kind of meat, these sausages are seasoned with fiery African Chakalaka salsa; it is made from onions, peppers, chiles, tomatoes, carrots, garlic, and curry powder.

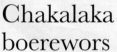

MEAT 🐂 and 🐖

TYPE Fresh

TYPICAL SIZE L: 28in (70cm), W: 1in (3cm)

SOUTH AFRICA Throughout, especially Johannesburg

Droëwors

A slim, quickly dried beef sausage. However, as they should contain very little fat, ostrich or game meat is also popular. The meat is uncured, but homemade versions sometimes use vinegar to prevent spoilage, which adds to the flavor. They are usually spicy, but not hot.

MEAT 🐂 or 🦢

TYPE Dried

TYPICAL SIZE L: 24in (60cm), W: ¾in (2cm)

SOUTH AFRICA Throughout

Springbok boerewors

Springbok meat is usually described as venison, although this dainty animal is not a deer. But its lean, rich, dark meat is similar to venison, and these sausages are filling and healthy.

MEAT 🦌

TYPE Fresh

TYPICAL SIZE L: 5in (12cm), W: 1in (3cm)

SOUTH AFRICA Throughout, especially Karoo

UNITED STATES OF AMERICA AND CANADA

The sausages of North America came over with its settlers, so the most common types in each area reveal the original country of its immigrant population: Polish, German, Scandinavian, French, or British. All these immigrant populations have distinct areas of settlement, as well as Italian and Chinese.

However, many of these pioneering sausages have evolved into something different from their Old World counterparts, so visitors to North America may find that sausages do not always correspond to the version they are used to at home. Although the hog reigns supreme when it comes to sausages, many sausages also come in kosher varieties made from beef or poultry.

People speak fondly of childhood memories featuring their family's favorite sausages—they are backyard barbecue food, street food, and the sausage, humble though it may be, remains an essential part of the North American celebration.

Andouille

Unlike French andouille, this slim, hot-smoked sausage is made from minced pork and smoked ham, not tripe. It is well spiced with black and cayenne pepper; the original Louisiana version is smokiest and best.

MEAT	🐷
TYPE	Cooked
TYPICAL SIZE	L: 5 in (12cm), W: 1 in (3cm)
USA	Throughout, especially Louisiana

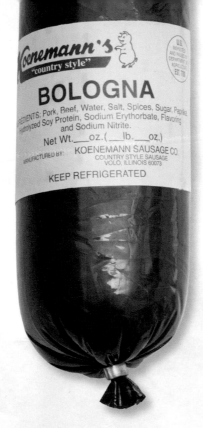

Koenemann's
"country style"

BOLOGNA

INGREDIENTS: Pork, Beef, Water, Salt, Spices, Sugar, Paprika, Hydrolyzed Soy Protein, Sodium Erythorbate, Flavoring and Sodium Nitrite.

Net Wt.___oz.(___lb.___oz.)

MANUFACTURED BY: KOENEMANN SAUSAGE CO.
COUNTRY STYLE SAUSAGE
VOLO, ILLINOIS 60073

KEEP REFRIGERATED

Blood sausage

A speciality item featured by ethnic butchers, American blood sausages differ according to the original immigrants' version, with German, British, Polish, and French being the most common types.

MEAT

TYPE Cooked

TYPICAL SIZE L: 5in (12cm), W: 2in (5cm)

USA AND CANADA Throughout

Bologna

Also called boloney (mortadella in Canada), this luncheon meat sausage is made from pork, beef, or poultry, and can be smoked. In the south, it is popular as fried breakfast meat.

MEAT and/or

TYPE Cooked

TYPICAL SIZE L: 12in (30cm), W: 4in (10cm)

USA AND CANADA Throughout

Boudin

A popular Cajun white sausage that was originally made from pork, rice, fresh herbs, and onion, but now is made with any white meat, including turkey or seafood. Boudin rouge includes blood.

MEAT and

TYPE Fresh or cooked

TYPICAL SIZE L: 4in (10cm), W: 1½in (4cm)

USA Louisiana

123

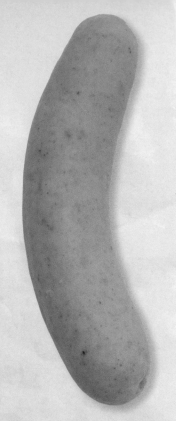

Bratwurst

A scalded pork sausage with a high fat content, usually cooked over charcoal. There are "beer and brat" festivals in Ontario and Wisconsin, where the "beer brat" is simmered in butter, onions, and lager beer, before being grilled.

MEAT 🐷

TYPE Fresh or cooked

TYPICAL SIZE L: 4in (10cm), W: 1in (3cm)

USA AND CANADA
Throughout, especially Wisconsin, Ohio, and Ontario

Breakfast sausage

A fresh, unsmoked sausage usually made from pork, though other meats are used as well. North Americans often enjoy them with maple syrup for breakfast. When puff pastry, pancakes, or dough are wrapped around them, they are called "pigs in blankets."

MEAT 🐷

TYPE Fresh

TYPICAL SIZE L: 4in (10cm), W: 1in (3cm)

USA AND CANADA
Throughout

Chorizo

Of the many types of chorizo made in the US, the Spanish style is a popular variety. Another favorite is spicy Mexican, or Tex-Mex, which is usually fresh. Louisiana chorizo is called chauriçe.

MEAT 🐷

TYPE Cured, or cured and dried

TYPICAL SIZE L: 8in (20cm), W: 1in (2.5cm)

USA AND CANADA
Throughout

Head cheese

The meat, skin, and tongue taken from a pig's head is slowly cooked and set into its own jelly, each meat providing a different texture. It can also be made from calf or lamb. It is eaten cold as a sliced luncheon meat.

MEAT or

TYPE Cooked

TYPICAL SIZE L: 8in (20cm), W: 5in (12cm)

USA AND CANADA
Throughout

Hot dog

Made from pork, poultry, beef, or veal, the many toppings vary from banana peppers to cheese and chiles. Whatever the regional variation, these are a must at every US sporting stadium.

MEAT or

TYPE Cooked

TYPICAL SIZE L: 6in (15cm), W: ¾in (2cm)

USA AND CANADA
Throughout

Italian sausage

A fresh, uncured pork sausage flavored with fennel seeds. There are both hot and sweet (mild) varieties; the hot one contains red chiles, the mild version often includes fresh basil.

MEAT

TYPE Fresh

TYPICAL SIZE L: 4in (10cm), W: 1¾in (4.5cm)

USA AND CANADA
Throughout

125

Kielbasa

This term can cover a wide variety of sausages but is generally used to describe the most common—a punchy, smoked garlic sausage made in the Central European style, usually presented in a ring.

MEAT 🐷

TYPE Cured and dried

TYPICAL SIZE L: 18in (45cm), W: 1½in (4cm)

USA AND CANADA Throughout

Liverwurst

Classed as a luncheon meat, this very smooth pâté contains pig's liver, pork or veal, and fat, and is cooked in a synthetic skin. It is spread on bread, and usually served with sweet or sharp dill pickles.

MEAT 🐷 and 🐑

TYPE Cooked

TYPICAL SIZE L: 7in (18cm), W: 2in (5cm)

USA AND CANADA Throughout

Pepperoni

A long, thin, dried salami made from pork and beef, well spiced with plenty of hot paprika, this is usually sliced and used for a pizza topping. There is also a larger version that is served as a luncheon meat.

MEAT 🐷 and 🐄

TYPE Cured and dried

TYPICAL SIZE L: 12in (30cm), W: ½in (1.5cm)

USA AND CANADA Throughout

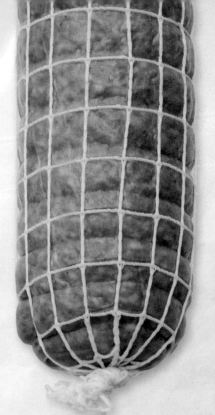

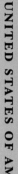

Pork sausage

Fresh pork sausage is the most widely eaten variety in North America, with many local variations of vegetable, herb, and spice mixtures. In Canada, a lightly smoked Mennonnite variety is a favorite.

MEAT 🐖

TYPE Fresh

TYPICAL SIZE L: 4in (10cm), W: 1in (3cm)

USA AND CANADA Throughout

Poultry sausage

Chicken and turkey are often regarded as alternatives to pork. The sausages can be pale, or quite dark if they are made from the leg meat. They can be mild or spicy.

MEAT 🦃 or 🦃

TYPE Fresh

TYPICAL SIZE L: 5in (12cm), W: 1in (3cm)

USA AND CANADA Throughout

Salami

The high number of Italian immigrants accounts for a wide variety of salami made throughout North America. Both dried and cooked (known as cotto) are made, usually in artificial casings. It is often smoked.

MEAT 🐖

TYPE Cured and dried, or cooked

TYPICAL SIZE L: 16in (40cm), W: 3in (8cm)

USA AND CANADA Throughout

127

Smoked sausage

Unlike kielbasa, which always contains garlic, smoked sausage is usually a generic name for a mild, smoked, cured pork sausage without garlic, but it can be either hot or cold smoked.

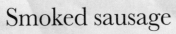

MEAT 🐷

TYPE Cured or cooked

TYPICAL SIZE L: 5in (12cm), W: 1in (3cm)

USA AND CANADA Throughout

Soy chorizo

A typical example of a vegetarian sausage, this Spanish-style "chorizo" is made from soybeans and is stuffed into synthetic skins. Paprika gives it flavor and characteristic orange color, and the mixture is cured.

VEGETARIAN

TYPE Cured

TYPICAL SIZE L: 8in (20cm), W: 1½in (4cm)

USA Throughout

Summer sausage

Summer sausage is made from mixed meats such as pork, beef, or venison. Its tangy flavor comes from the curing process, and it can be smoked or unsmoked. Usually eaten cold.

MEAT 🐷 and 🐷

TYPE Cured and dried

TYPICAL SIZE L: 12in (30cm), W: 2½in (6cm)

USA AND CANADA Throughout

Venison sausage

Very little is available commercially, but huge amounts are made at home from hunted deer and elk. Pork fat is often added for moisture, and they are often well spiced and smoked.

MEAT and

TYPE Fresh or dried

TYPICAL SIZE L: 6in (15cm), W: 1in (3cm)

USA AND CANADA Throughout

Weisswurst

Also called white bratwurst (white pudding in Canada), this very pale, mild, pork and veal sausage is fairly bready and crumbly. Cheaper versions are made from poultry. It is recooked before eating.

MEAT and

TYPE Cooked

TYPICAL SIZE L: 6in (15cm), W: 1in (3cm)

USA AND CANADA Throughout

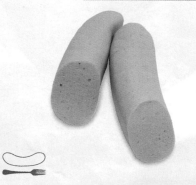

Wild boar salami

A gourmet sausage made in natural casings, the wild boar usually comes from ranches. The dark, lean meat has a rich flavor. It tends to be flavored with powerful spices such as juniper or cloves, and often includes red wine.

MEAT

TYPE Dried

TYPICAL SIZE L: 5in (12cm), W: 2in (5cm)

USA Throughout

CENTRAL AND SOUTH AMERICA

The sausages of **Central and South America are versions of chorizo, longaniza, morcela, and salami. While their names are familiar, these sausages are rarely the same as their Spanish, Portuguese, and Italian counterparts. Slightly confusingly, some of these names also represent completely different sausages in different countries. For example, hot dogs are called** *salchichas* **in Mexico, but in Argentina,** *salchichas* **are long lengths of fresh sausage; hot dogs are** *panchos.*

Having taken on characters of their own, all these sausages are nevertheless enjoyed in quintessentially South American style, with charcoal grills popular everywhere. Beef is used to a greater degree than in Europe, since so much is produced, and instead of paprika, the native chile is used extensively. Other ingredients included to give flavor and typical southern vibrancy are spinach, to produce brilliant green chorizos, and even strawberry juice, which make them bright red in color.

Chorizo Argentino

In Argentina, chorizo is any kind of fresh, coarse-grained sausage, usually of beef and pork. Some are tied with string, some are in links, and spices vary from mild to hot. They are eaten in the famous *choripan* (sausage in a roll).

MEAT 🐄 and 🐖

TYPE Fresh

TYPICAL SIZE L: 5in (12cm), W: 1in (3cm)

ARGENTINA Throughout

Chorizo Colombiano

A coarsely chopped pork (or sometimes beef) sausage, seasoned with paprika, garlic, coriander, cumin, marjoram, and pepper. *Chorizo Antioqueño* from the north is the most famous. It is eaten on white corn bread.

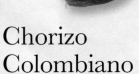

MEAT 🐷 or 🐖	
TYPE Cured	
TYPICAL SIZE L: 5in (12cm), W: 1½in (4cm)	
COLOMBIA Throughout, especially Antioquia	

Chorizo Mexicano

Mexican chorizo is usually a cured, undried pork or chicken sausage, with plenty of red poblano chile. The most famous come from Toluca, where they are tied into links with corn husks. Some are quite crumbly and eaten on tostadas.

MEAT 🐷 or 🐓	
TYPE Cured	
TYPICAL SIZE L: 7in (18cm), W: 1½in (4cm)	
MEXICO Throughout, especially Toluca	

Chorizo Salvadoreño

Salvadorean chorizo is usually spicy with coriander and chile, and often colored with paprika and *achiote*: a natural yellow coloring. The most famous come from Cojutepeque, where the ends are tied with corn husks.

MEAT 🐷 and 🐄	
TYPE Cured	
TYPICAL SIZE L: 5in (12cm), W: 1in (3cm)	
EL SALVADOR Throughout, especially Cojutepeque	

131

Chorizo verde

This unusual green chorizo varies in color depending on the amount of vegetables it contains. It is made from pork, chiles, spinach, cilantro, parsley, green peppercorns, and oregano. Some versions include tomatillos, pine nuts, or almonds.

MEAT 🐗

TYPE Fresh

TYPICAL SIZE L: 4in (10cm), W: 1in (3cm)

MEXICO Throughout, especially Toluca

Linguiça

Linguiça arrived in Brazil during the Portuguese colonial period. It is made from lean pork, robustly seasoned with garlic and paprika, and then cured; unlike Portuguese *linguiça*, it is not usually dried. It is an important feature of the *churrascaria* (barbecue).

MEAT 🐗

TYPE Cured

TYPICAL SIZE L: 17in (43cm), W: 1½in (4cm)

BRAZIL Throughout

Longaniza

A long, slim sausage made in the fermented chorizo style. Most versions are dried, some are smoked, and others are flavored with anise, giving them a very distinctive taste. It is usually eaten raw and sliced like salami; it is not often cooked.

MEAT 🐗

TYPE Cured and dried

TYPICAL SIZE L: 9in (23cm), W: 1½in (4cm)

ARGENTINA, BRAZIL, MEXICO, AND URUGUAY Throughout

132

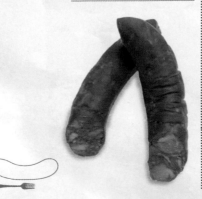

Morcela/morcilla

Blood sausages in various forms are popular throughout the region. Known as *morcela* in Brazil and *morcilla* in Argentina, they are also called *moronga* (Mexico), *relleno* (Argentina, Peru), or *chouriço de sangue* (Brazil). They can be freshly made or dried. Some are mild, others hot and spicy.

MEAT	🐷
TYPE	Cooked
TYPICAL SIZE	L: 12in (30cm), W: 1in (3cm)
CENTRAL AND SOUTH AMERICA	Throughout

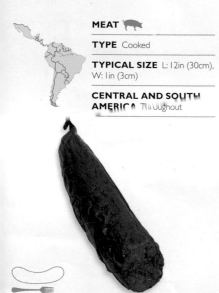

Panchos

These are Argentina's name for hot dog sausages, and are common street food throughout the country. In Mexico, hot dog sausages are known as *salchichas*, where this word also means crumbly sausages that are removed from the skin and eaten on tostadas.

MEAT	🐷
TYPE	Cooked
TYPICAL SIZE	L: 7in (18cm), W: 1in (1.5cm)
ARGENTINA	Throughout

Salchichas parilleras

A long, fresh sausage made into a large coil secured with skewers. They are usually made from a beef and pork mixture, with pepper, sugar, wine, and sweet paprika. They are grilled on charcoal barbecues (*parilleras*).

MEAT	🐄 and 🐷
TYPE	Fresh
TYPICAL SIZE	L: 39in (1m), W: 1in (3cm)
ARGENTINA	Throughout

133

ASIA

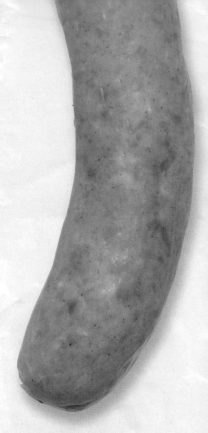

Asia covers an enormous area, but in terms of sausages it falls into three categories. Sausages in the Indian subcontinent are mostly versions of either Portuguese or British sausages; they retain those characteristics but with a deliciously spicy Indian twist. In South Asia, many sausages are fermented, which gives them a very distinctive sour-sweet taste. The flavorings of this region are typically fragrant, including lemongrass, galangal, chile, fish paste, kaffir lime, mint, palm sugar, and star anise.

The sausages of China are categorized in several different ways, which can be confusing. Some are named according to their regional characteristics (such as Hunan or Sichuan). Others are named according to their main ingredient (such as liver, sticky rice, lemon, prawn, egg yolk, starch, etc.). *La chang* or *lap cheong* are generic words for "sausage"—these are usually made from hand-chopped meat. They are slim and were originally wind dried in the cool winter months, traditionally around the Chinese New Year.

Beijing garlic sausage

A typical snack on the streets of Beijing, this sausage is made from pork mixed with starch and seasonings. It is put into pork casings and boiled. Once cool, it is sliced, fried, and served with garlic sauce.

MEAT 🐖

TYPE Cooked

TYPICAL SIZE L: 6in (15cm), W: 1½in (3.5cm)

CHINA Beijing

Fen chang

The principal ingredients of this sausage are pork and bean starch, with scallion, sesame oil, soy, ginger, and pepper. It is cured, boiled with a little brown sugar, and then lightly smoked.

MEAT

TYPE Cooked

TYPICAL SIZE L: 16in (40cm), W: 2in (5cm)

CHINA Tianjin

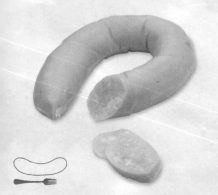

Goan chorizo

These pork or beef sausages hail from when Goa was a Portuguese colony. They are spiced with turmeric, cumin, hot paprika, and garlic. They are fermented and may be smoked and dried. "Goan sausage" usually refers to linguiça. Other Indian sausages are British-style with Indian spicing.

MEAT or

TYPE Cured, or cured and dried

TYPICAL SIZE L: 3in (8cm), W: 1in (2.5cm)

INDIA Goa, Daman, and Diu

Guangdong sausage

The characteristic flavor is a salty sweetness. Usually made from coarse-cut pork, these sausages can also be made from duck, chicken, seafood, or mushrooms. They are air dried and steamed over rice, or sliced and stir fried.

MEAT or

TYPE Dried

TYPICAL SIZE L: 6½in (17cm), W: ½in (1.5cm)

CHINA Guangzhou, Guangdong

135

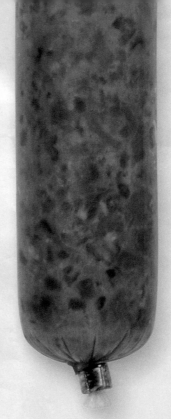

Harbin hongchang

This dark red sausage is not typically Chinese but is a popular one. Made from pork studded with small cubes of pork fat, it is made in the German style. Both fermented and smoked, it has a tangy, savory flavor.

MEAT 🐷

TYPE Cured and dried

TYPICAL SIZE L: 7in (18cm), W: 1in (3cm)

CHINA Harbin, Northeast

Naem moo

A slim sausage made with pork, pork skin, and glutinous rice, intensely flavored with garlic and chiles. It is fermented—traditionally in banana leaves—which makes it taste tangy, and is served raw, in slices with shallots, peanuts, and sliced ginger. Also known as *som moo* (Laos) or *nem chua* (Vietnam).

MEAT 🐷

TYPE Cured

TYPICAL SIZE L: 8in (20cm), W: 1in (3cm)

THAILAND, LAOS, AND VIETNAM Throughout

Sai krok Isan

Originating from the Isan region of northeast Thailand, these small, round sausages are made from pork and fermented glutinous rice, flavored with garlic and ginger. They are cooked in strings. First steamed then charcoal grilled, they are doused in coconut milk and served with fragrant vegetables.

MEAT 🐷

TYPE Cured

TYPICAL SIZE L: 1½in (4cm), W: 1in (3cm)

THAILAND Northeast

Sai oua

These small, pale sausages are made from pork and pork skin, with a large proportion of glutinous rice flavored with garlic, lemongrass, and galangal. They are fermented, which gives them a rich, sour taste. They are first boiled and then grilled.

MEAT

TYPE Cured

TYPICAL SIZE L: 1½in (4cm), W: 1in (2.5cm)

LAOS AND VIETNAM Throughout

Sichuan sausage

A coarsely chopped sausage normally made with fatty pork, this wind-dried sausage is seasoned with both chile and Sichuan pepper so it is hot and spicy rather than sweet. They are sometimes smoked before being steamed or boiled.

MEAT

TYPE Cured and dried

TYPICAL SIZE L: 9½in (24cm), W: 1in (3cm)

CHINA Sichuan

Sundae

Usually made with pig or cattle blood and noodles, although some of the many versions use fish. The noodles give jelly-like texture. They are flavored with garlic, scallions, and fragrant herbs. It is served with *Ddukbokki*: spicy rice cakes.

MEAT or

TYPE Cooked

TYPICAL SIZE L: 39in (1m), W: 1½in (4cm)

KOREA Throughout

AUSTRALIA AND NEW ZEALAND

Ask an Australian or a New Zealander for examples of their countries' sausages, and they look puzzled. "We don't really have any," they say. In one sense this is true, since indigenous Māori and Aboriginal cooking does not include sausages.

But in fact these Pacific Rim countries have a wealth of different flavors and styles of sausages that have been brought over by immigrants during the last 200 years. For a long time, sausages were almost exclusively British in style, fresh and bound with twice-baked biscuits, or made in the saveloy or hot dog style. They were regarded as providing a cheap and cheerful meal, and this is reflected in their slang names: snags, snarlers, or bangers.

Today, although sausages are still essential for the "barbie" or sausage sizzle (street vendor), they are becoming increasingly sophisticated, reflecting the influence of Europe and Asia, where sausages are taken very seriously and are made from high-quality ingredients.

Beef sausage

Made fresh in the British style, there are dozens of different added flavors such as red wine, mustard, or even *kawakawa* (Māori bush basil). In the parts of New Zealand colonized by Scots, beef sausages are still preferred to pork.

MEAT

TYPE Fresh

TYPICAL SIZE L: 8in (20cm), W: 1½in (3.5cm)

AUSTRALIA AND NEW ZEALAND
Throughout

Cheerios

Bright red and highly spiced, cheerios are small, cocktail-sized saveloys that are a popular and essential part of children's parties in both Australia and New Zealand. Although there was a tradition of eating them cold, they are now generally reheated.

MEAT

TYPE Cooked

TYPICAL SIZE L: 3in (8cm), W: 1in (2.5cm)

AUSTRALIA AND NEW ZEALAND Throughout

Chorizo

A popular example of the international influences on the sausages made in these two Pacific Rim countries. Very often they are still fresh sausages, rather than being cured or dried, but made with foreign spices. Others include *bratwurst, hmong, horiatiko*, and *sucuk*, or Chinese and Thai-style sausages.

MEAT

TYPE Fresh, or cured and dried

TYPICAL SIZE L: 6in (15cm), W: 1½in (3.5cm)

AUSTRALIA AND NEW ZEALAND Throughout

Devon sausage

Also called Polony or Luncheon sausage, this is a large, cooked, slicing sausage used as a cheap snack, usually eaten in a sandwich or bun, with tomato ketchup. The sausage and the name Polony are derived from Bologna sausage.

MEAT

TYPE Cooked

TYPICAL SIZE L: 20in (50cm), W: 4½in (11cm)

AUSTRALIA AND NEW ZEALAND Throughout

139

Kabana

Also called cabanossi, these cured, smoked, and partly dried sausages are flavored with garlic, and made in a similar way to Polish sausages. As well as being barbecued, they are also served sliced, and served cold with cheese as an appetizer.

MEAT

TYPE Cured and dried

TYPICAL SIZE L: 16in (40cm), W: 1in (2.5cm)

AUSTRALIA AND NEW ZEALAND Throughout

Kangaroo sausage

Affectionately known as "kanga bangers", these are surely the iconic Australian sausage. Kangaroo meat looks and tastes similar to wild venison, so the sausages are dark in color and powerful in flavor. The best are made with natural casings.

MEAT

TYPE Fresh

TYPICAL SIZE L: 5in (13cm), W: 1½in (4cm)

AUSTRALIA Throughout

Lamb sausage

Fresh lamb sausages tend to be flavored with herbs such as rosemary, mint, thyme, or basil, and will usually contain a binder of twice-baked biscuits. Lamb is also made into *merguez*- or *sucuk*-style sausages. Both countries are renowned for their sheep production.

MEAT

TYPE Fresh

TYPICAL SIZE L: 5in (13cm), W: 1½in (4cm)

AUSTRALIA AND NEW ZEALAND Throughout

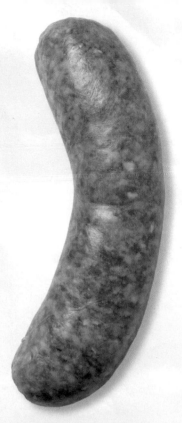

Pork sausage

An essential part of the sausage sizzle, pork sausages are made in the British fashion, though there are dozens of different flavorings. In Australia, a "hot dog" served in a long roll will be this type of fresh sausage rather than a saveloy.

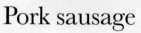

MEAT 🐖

TYPE Fresh

TYPICAL SIZE L: 6¼in (16cm), W: 1¾in (4.5cm)

AUSTRALIA AND NEW ZEALAND Throughout

Saveloy

Australian saveloys tend to be made with inexpensive ingredients. If served battered on a stick, they are called a "battered sav." New Zealand "savs" are larger, and made with more expensive ingredients. They are often sold raw to cook at home.

MEAT 🐖

TYPE Fresh or cooked

TYPICAL SIZE L: 8in (20cm), W: ¾in (2cm)

AUSTRALIA AND NEW ZEALAND Throughout

Venison sausage

Venison sausages are available commercially as a result of New Zealand's flourishing deer farming industry, though they are also made in Australia. Darker in color, and leaner than beef sausages, they are usually fresh, but venison is also made into salami.

MEAT 🦌

TYPE Fresh or dried

TYPICAL SIZE L: 6in (15cm), W: 1in (2.5cm)

NEW ZEALAND Throughout

141

Enjoying and Making Sausages

Nürnberger Rostbratwurst with parsley potatoes and sauerkraut

This thin sausage from Nuremburg, Germany, is one of the country's favorites, perhaps due to its traditional seasoning of fresh marjoram. Simply grill or pan-fry to enjoy it as the Germans do. This recipe makes a quick dinner dish, with the piquant sauerkraut and hot horseradish lifting the whole plate.

SERVES 4

PREP 10 MINS

COOK 30 MINS

INGREDIENTS

1–2 tsp fresh horseradish, grated, to taste, or 2 tbsp creamed horseradish

⅔ cup sour cream

salt and freshly ground black pepper

8–12 Nürnberger Rostbratwurst, or enough to serve 4

2–4 tbsp olive oil

1 large onion, finely diced

1lb 5oz (600g) new potatoes, peeled, cooked, and cut into ¾in (2cm) dice

2 tbsp finely chopped flat-leaf parsley

10–14oz (300–400g) sauerkraut, or enough to serve 4

SAUSAGE ALTERNATIVES
• Pork and beef chipolatas
• French fresh saucisse

1 Fold the horseradish into the sour cream. Season well and set aside. Pierce the sausages all over with a fork, and grill or cook them over low heat for 10 minutes, until well cooked and browned all over.

2 Meanwhile, heat the olive oil in a large frying pan over medium heat, and cook the onion for about 5 minutes, until softened but not brown. Add the potatoes and cook for 5–7 minutes, until golden brown on all sides. Add the parsley, and season.

3 Place the sauerkraut in a small, heavy saucepan, and gently heat, stirring occasionally, until warmed through.

4 Serve the sausages with the potatoes and sauerkraut, with the horseradish cream on the side.

Boerewors, mieliepap, and sauce

Boerewors is usually grilled on a barbecue, or *braai*, in South Africa, but it can just as easily be fried. It is traditionally served with mieliepap, a corn porridge. Add grated or shaved Parmesan to the polenta before serving for variation.

SERVES 4

PREP 15 MINS

COOK 40 MINS

INGREDIENTS

8 boerewors, or enough to serve 4 if in the traditional coil (1¾–2lb (800–900g))

For the mieliepap

1 quart chicken or beef stock

7oz (200g) coarse polenta

salt and freshly ground black pepper

2 tbsp unsalted butter

2 tbsp finely chopped flat-leaf parsley

For the sauce

2 tbsp olive oil

1 onion, finely chopped

2 garlic cloves, crushed

4 ripe tomatoes, peeled and finely chopped

1 tbsp tomato paste

½ tsp granulated sugar (optional)

a few drops of Tabasco, to taste

SAUSAGE ALTERNATIVES

• Cumberland sausage
• Saucisse de Toulouse
• Luganega

1 In a large, heavy saucepan, bring the stock to a gentle simmer. Put the polenta in a liquid measuring cup or small pitcher and pour it into the stock in a thin stream, whisking all the time so it does not clump. Season well and bring to a boil. Reduce the heat to a very low simmer and cook for 20 minutes, stirring, until it begins to come away from the sides of the pan.

2 Meanwhile, heat the oil in a heavy saucepan over low heat. Add the onion and cook for 5 minutes, until softened. Add the garlic, tomatoes, tomato paste, sugar (if using), Tabasco, and ⅔ cup water and season well. Bring to a boil, reduce the heat, and simmer for 15 minutes until thickened.

3 Broil, barbecue, or pan-fry the boerewors over medium heat for about 15 minutes, until cooked, browned, and crispy. Stir the butter and parsley into the mieliepap and serve with the sauce poured over and the boerewors on the side.

Boerewors
Beef and vinegar make this highly flavored, coiled sausage wonderful grilled on the barbecue.

New York hot dogs with quick sauerkraut

New Yorkers like an all-beef (often kosher) hot dog, served with sauerkraut and spicy mustard. This recipe for quick sauerkraut is a great substitute for the long-fermented original.

SERVES 4

(SAUERKRAUT SERVES 4 AS A SIDE DISH, AND MORE AS A HOT DOG ACCOMPANIMENT)

PREP 10 MINS

COOK 40 MINS

INGREDIENTS

2 tbsp vegetable or sunflower oil

2 tbsp unsalted butter, plus extra to serve

1 onion, halved and finely sliced

10oz (300g) green cabbage (trimmed weight), quartered and finely sliced

½ tsp caraway seeds, lightly crushed

1 tsp granulated sugar

salt and freshly ground black pepper

⅓ cup white wine vinegar

1¼ cups apple juice

8 all-beef (kosher or halal are good) hot dogs, or enough to serve 4

8 soft hot dog rolls, or enough to serve 4

spicy mustard, to serve

SAUSAGE ALTERNATIVES
• Wiener Würstel
• Regensburger
• Saucisse de Strasbourg

1 In a large, heavy saucepan, heat the oil and butter together. Add the onion and cabbage and cook over low heat for 5 minutes, until softened and wilted. Add the caraway seeds and sugar, and season well. Add the vinegar and apple juice, and bring to a boil.

2 Reduce the heat to a low simmer, cover, and cook for 30 minutes, until the cabbage is soft. Remove the lid, increase the heat, and cook the cabbage for 5 minutes, until the liquid has reduced. Check the seasoning, and stir in the butter.

3 Meanwhile, to cook the hot dogs, bring a large pan of water to a boil. Add the hot dogs, reduce the heat, and simmer gently for about 5 minutes, until heated through. Serve inside the split rolls with the quick sauerkraut and some spicy mustard on the side.

Hot dog
Very finely ground meat gives this a smooth texture. Best in a roll with spicy condiments.

Sausage and butterbean goulash

This recipe works best with a variety of German-style cooked or scalded sausages. It is conservatively spiced, but feel free to increase the amount of cayenne pepper and smoked paprika for a more vibrant flavor. If you prefer, use your favorite white beans or chickpeas, instead of butterbeans.

SERVES 4

PREP 10 MINS

COOK 35 MINS

INGREDIENTS

2 tbsp olive oil

1 onion, finely chopped

1 red bell pepper, seeded, and cut into ¾in (2cm) cubes

1 yellow bell pepper, seeded, and cut into ¾in (2cm) cubes

2 garlic cloves, crushed

1 tbsp all-purpose flour

½ tsp cayenne pepper

½ tsp smoked paprika

14fl oz (400ml) tomato sauce

1¼ cups chicken stock

salt and freshly ground black pepper

14oz (400g) mixed wurst, such as Krakauer, Bockwurst, and Lyoner Fleischwurst, skinned if necessary, and cut into ¾in (2cm) chunks

14oz (400g) can butterbeans, drained and rinsed

2 tbsp finely chopped flat-leaf parsley

2 tbsp sour cream

SAUSAGE ALTERNATIVES

- Bratwurst
- Parówka
- Saucisse Viennoise

1 In a large, heavy saucepan, heat the oil over low heat and gently cook the onion and peppers for 5 minutes until softened, but not browned. Add the garlic and cook for 2 more minutes.

2 Stir in the flour, cayenne pepper, and smoked paprika, and stir well. Add the tomato sauce and chicken stock to the pan, and mix thoroughly. Season with salt and pepper if needed (the stock may be salty). Bring to a boil, reduce the heat, and simmer for 10 minutes.

3 Add the wurst and continue to simmer for 10 minutes. Add the butterbeans and gently simmer for a final 5 minutes.

4 Stir in the parsley and serve with the sour cream swirled on top, or on the side, with white rice or crusty bread.

Bockwurst
The gentle spicing of this mild sausage lends itself to comforting stews and braises.

Tomato and chorizo soup

This easy and delicious light dinner or lunch dish showcases the spiciness of chorizo. Make sure you use the best chorizo you can find. If you like, you can make a double batch of this soup, and freeze half for another day. It will keep for up to three months in the freezer.

SERVES 8

PREP 20 MINS

COOK 40 MINS

INGREDIENTS

2 tbsp olive oil

9oz (250g) Spanish chorizo, in small cubes

2 red onions, finely chopped

4 celery stalks, finely chopped

4 carrots, finely chopped

3 garlic cloves, grated or finely chopped

salt and freshly ground black pepper

24oz (700g) can tomato sauce

1 quart hot vegetable stock

2 x 14oz (400g) cans chickpeas, drained and rinsed

handful of fresh cilantro, finely chopped, to serve

SAUSAGE ALTERNATIVES
• Merguez
• Kiełbasa zwyczajna
• Salame Sardo

1 Heat half the oil in a large, heavy pan. Add the chorizo, and cook over medium heat, stirring occasionally, for 5 minutes, or until it begins to turn crispy. Remove and set aside.

2 Heat the remaining oil in the pan, add the onions, and cook over low heat for 6–8 minutes, or until soft and translucent. Stir in the celery, carrots, and garlic, and season with salt and pepper. Cook over low heat, stirring occasionally, for 8 minutes, or until tender.

3 Add the tomato sauce, stock, and chickpeas, and simmer for 15 minutes. Return the chorizo to the pan, then taste and season again if needed. Stir through the cilantro, and serve.

Pea and sausage soup

Warming and perfect for a chilly day, enjoy this hearty soup with slices of dark German rye bread and a glass of white wine or wheat beer. The base of the pea soup takes very well to other flavorings, so try smoked sausages, or even spicy sausages, such as chorizo.

SERVES 6

PREP 20 MINS

COOK 20 MINS

INGREDIENTS

2 tbsp unsalted butter

1 large carrot, chopped

1 small leek, chopped

2 celery stalks, chopped

1 potato, chopped

leaves from ½ bunch flat-leaf parsley, chopped

½ cup dry white wine

1 quart hot chicken stock

10oz (300g) saucisse de Toulouse

1lb 10oz (750g) peas (frozen or fresh)

salt and freshly ground black pepper

SAUSAGE ALTERNATIVES

• Luganega
• Chorizo
• Boerewors

1 Preheat the oven to 350°F (180°C). In a large saucepan, melt the butter and cook the carrot, leek, celery, and potato, stirring until softened. Add the parsley, wine, and stock, and simmer for 15 minutes.

2 Place the sausages on a baking sheet and cook, turning occasionally, for 15–20 minutes, or until cooked through and golden brown on all sides. Slice and set aside.

3 Add the peas to the pot and cook for 3–4 minutes, or until just al dente. Season and process to a purée in a blender. Return to the pot and heat through. Serve in warmed bowls, garnished with the sliced sausage.

Stuffed cabbage leaves with creamy mustard sauce

Although traditionally a winter dish, these little parcels are surprisingly light and delicate. The mustard sauce is the perfect foil with its slightly tangy taste. Serve with some creamy mashed potatoes for the ultimate in comfort food.

SERVES 4

PREP 20 MINS

COOK 1 HR

SPECIAL EQUIPMENT
OVENPROOF DISH

INGREDIENTS

8 outer leaves of a Savoy cabbage

salt and freshly ground black pepper

2 tbsp light olive oil

½ onion, finely chopped

1 carrot, finely chopped

½ celery stalk, trimmed and chopped

2½oz (75g) mushrooms, trimmed and finely chopped

1 tbsp finely chopped sage

1 garlic clove, crushed

4 pork and leek sausages (about 2½oz (75g) each), skinned

½ apple, peeled, cored, and grated

3½oz (100g) fresh white bread crumbs

½ large egg, beaten

good grating of nutmeg

1¾ cups chicken stock

½ cup apple juice

2 tbsp crème fraîche

1 heaping tsp Dijon mustard

SAUSAGE ALTERNATIVES
• Saucisse de Toulouse
• Luganega
• Breakfast sausage

1 Preheat the oven to 400°F (200°C). In a large saucepan, plunge the cabbage into boiling, salted water, and cook for 1–2 minutes, until the leaves are pliable. Drain, and cut out the central ribs, keeping the leaves as intact as possible.

2 In a large frying pan, heat the oil. Add the onion, carrot, and celery, and cook until softened. Add the mushrooms and cook for 2–3 minutes. Add the sage and garlic, and cook for 2–3 minutes more.

3 Crumble the sausages into a bowl. Mix in the cooked vegetables, apple, bread crumbs, egg, nutmeg, and seasoning.

4 Place the cabbage leaves on a cutting board. Divide the stuffing between each, and fold in the sides. Pack the parcels, join downward, into an ovenproof dish in a single layer. Heat the stock and apple juice together in a saucepan, and pour over the parcels. Cover with foil, and cook in the oven for 40 minutes.

5 Drain the liquid into a frying pan over high heat. Reduce until it just covers the bottom of the pan. Stir in the crème fraîche and mustard, season, then pour the sauce over the parcels to serve.

Pork and leek sausage
Leeks and pork are a perfect flavor pairing.
This slightly oniony sausage is best with mustard.

Game sausages, celery root gratin, and braised red cabbage

This hearty dish delivers all the tastes and textures you could want on a cold winter's night. The cabbage can be reheated several times, so make plenty of it and store it in the refrigerator. If celery root is not available, try using waxy potatoes.

SERVES 4

PREP 25 MINS

COOK 2 HRS

SPECIAL EQUIPMENT
LARGE HEAVY FLAMEPROOF CASSEROLE; LARGE SHALLOW OVENPROOF DISH

INGREDIENTS

8–12 fresh game sausages, such as venison, enough for 4 servings

For the red cabbage

4 tbsp unsalted butter

2 tbsp granulated sugar

1 tsp salt

6 tbsp rice wine vinegar, white wine vinegar, or cider vinegar

1 red cabbage, finely shredded (about 2¼lb (1kg))

2 sweet apples, peeled, cored, and grated

2 heaping tbsp red currant jelly

For the gratin

2 tbsp unsalted butter, softened

1½lb (650g) celery root (trimmed weight), peeled and thinly sliced

2 garlic cloves, crushed

salt and freshly ground black pepper

1¾ cup half and half

SAUSAGE ALTERNATIVES
• Wild boar sausage
• Kangaroo sausage
• Saucisse de cheval

1 Preheat the oven to 325°F (160°C). For the cabbage, in a large, heavy, flameproof casserole, heat the butter, sugar, salt, vinegar, and 6 tablespoons of water. Bring to a boil, and simmer for 1 minute.

2 Fold in the cabbage, and return to a boil. Cover tightly with 2 layers of foil and the lid, and cook in the oven for 2 hours, on the lowest rack. After 1½ hours, stir in the apples and jelly, adding water if it looks dry. Replace the foil and lid, and return to the oven for the remaining 30 minutes.

3 Meanwhile, for the gratin, lightly grease a large, shallow, ovenproof dish with butter, and layer in half the celery root. Sprinkle with the garlic, season, and layer in the remaining celery root. Pour over the half and half and dot with the remaining butter.

4 Cook in the top of the oven for 1¼ hours, until soft when pierced with a knife.

5 Grill the sausages for 5–10 minutes, turning, until browned all over. Serve with the gratin and cabbage.

Venison sausage
A definite gamey taste makes this great in a wintry stew of red wine and root vegetables.

Cumberland sausages with roasted root vegetables

This delightfully simple recipe allows the ingredients to shine. The root vegetables melt in the mouth, and perfectly complement the coarse-textured sausage. Each Cumberland sausage should be big enough to feed one person, but allow more if you find smaller ones.

SERVES 4

PREP 10 MINS

COOK 50–55 MINS

INGREDIENTS

10oz (300g) butternut squash, peeled, seeded, and cut into bite-sized chunks

1 large or 2 small leeks, cut into 1in (3cm) pieces

2 small red onions, quartered

10oz (300g) small new potatoes, scrubbed, and halved lengthwise (quartered if large)

¼ cup olive oil, plus extra for the sausages

salt and freshly ground black pepper

2 tbsp thyme leaves

1 tbsp chopped rosemary leaves

4 Cumberland sausage coils, each weighing about 7oz (200g), or 8 Cumberland sausages, weighing 3½oz (100g) each

SAUSAGE ALTERNATIVES
• Luganega
• French fresh saucisse
• Any fresh pork sausage, such as breakfast sausage

1 Preheat the oven to 400°F (200°C). Spread out the butternut squash, leeks, onions, and new potatoes in a large roasting pan big enough to fit them in a single layer. Drizzle over the oil, season, and scatter with the herbs.

2 Toss the vegetables in the oil until well coated. Cook in the top third of the oven for 20 minutes.

3 Pierce the sausages several times on each side to prevent them from bursting in the oven, rub a little oil on each, and place them on top of the vegetables before returning them to the oven.

4 After 15 minutes, remove the sausages, and turn the vegetables. Replace the sausages on top, the other way up from their first cooking, and cook the whole dish for a final 15–20 minutes, or until everything is well browned.

Sausage rolls

These bite-sized rolls are perfect for parties or packed lunches, and are usually very popular with children. You can also make them well in advance. Unbaked, they will freeze for up to three months. They are especially good with a spicy mustard and crème fraîche dipping sauce.

MAKES 24

PREP 30 MINS, PLUS CHILLING

COOK 10–12 MINS

INGREDIENTS

14oz (400g) ready-made puff pastry, thawed if frozen

1½lb (675g) good-quality fresh pork sausages

1 small onion, finely chopped

1 tbsp chopped thyme leaves

1 tbsp finely grated lemon zest

1 tsp Dijon mustard

1 egg yolk, plus 1 whole egg, beaten, for glazing

salt and freshly ground black pepper

all-purpose flour, for dusting

SAUSAGE ALTERNATIVES
• Saucisse de Toulouse
• Luganega
• Boerewors

1 Preheat the oven to 400°F (200°C). Line a baking sheet with waxed paper and chill. Cut the puff pastry in half lengthwise. Roll each piece out to form a 12 x 6in (30 x 15cm) rectangle, then cover with plastic wrap and chill.

2 Slit the sausages and squeeze the meat into a bowl. Discard the skins. Combine the sausage with the onion, thyme, lemon zest, mustard, and egg yolk, and season with salt and pepper.

3 Remove the pastry from the refrigerator and lay the pieces on a floured surface. Roll the sausage mixture into 2 thin tubes and place one in the center of each piece of pastry. Brush the inside of the pastry with the beaten egg, then roll the pastry over and press to seal. Cut each roll into 12 pieces.

4 Place the rolls on the chilled sheet, make 2 snips in the top of each with scissors, then brush with beaten egg. Bake for 10–12 minutes, or until golden and flaky. Serve warm, or transfer to a wire rack to cool before serving.

Toad in the hole

A true British classic. Once you've mastered the basic recipe, try experimenting. Wrap bacon strips around the sausages before baking, or put whole-grain mustard in the batter. Or try it with your favorite fresh sausage. However you make it, toad in the hole is best served with onion gravy.

SERVES 4

PREP 15 MINS

COOK 40 MINS

SPECIAL EQUIPMENT
OVENPROOF DISH

INGREDIENTS

1 cup all-purpose flour

salt and freshly ground black pepper

2 large eggs

1¼ cups milk

a few sage leaves, chopped

8 good-quality fresh pork sausages, such as Lincolnshire sausages

1 tbsp olive oil

SAUSAGE ALTERNATIVES
• Italian sausage (American)
• Fresh lamb sausage
• Medister pølse

1 Sift the flour into a bowl with a pinch of salt. Create a well in the center, crack in the eggs, and pour in a little of the milk. Stir with a wooden spoon until well combined. Gradually add the remaining milk, beating all the time, until you have a smooth batter. (You may find it easier to use a whisk.)

2 Season the batter and stir in the sage. Leave the batter in the refrigerator to rest. Preheat the oven to 400°F (200°C).

3 Put the sausages into an ovenproof dish. Drizzle with the oil, and cook in the oven for 15–20 minutes, until the sausages are golden.

4 Remove the dish from the oven, and carefully pour over the batter. Return to the oven, and cook for about 15 minutes more until the batter is risen and golden. Serve with mashed potatoes and onion gravy.

Cocido

A classic Spanish one-pot meal, this is a fabulously warming dish for a bitterly cold night. There are a lot of different meats here, but make sure the chorizo and morcilla you choose are of good quality.

SERVES 6–8

PREP 25 MINS

COOK 2 HRS 45 MINS

INGREDIENTS

4 tbsp olive oil

4 small onions, quartered

2 garlic cloves, sliced

4 thick slices belly pork, about 1lb 2oz (500g) in total

4 chicken thighs, about 10oz (300g) in total

9oz (250g) beef braising steak, cut into 4 slices

6oz (175g) tocino or smoked bacon, cut into 4 pieces

4 small pork spare ribs, 5½oz (150g) total

3½fl oz (100ml) white wine

6oz (175g) chorizo, cut into 4 pieces

6oz (175g) morcilla

1 small ham bone

1 bay leaf

salt and freshly ground black pepper

8 small waxy potatoes

4 carrots, peeled and halved lengthwise

14oz (400g) can chickpeas, drained

1 Savoy cabbage or green cabbage heart, quartered

3 tbsp chopped flat-leaf parsley, to garnish

SAUSAGE ALTERNATIVES
• Instead of chorizo: merguez, or salame Sardo
• Instead of morcilla: boudin noir, or Schwarzwurst

1 Heat 1 tablespoon of oil in a large saucepan with the onions and garlic, and cook for 10 minutes, stirring occasionally. Heat the remaining oil in a frying pan and cook the pork, chicken, beef, tocino, and spare ribs in batches until lightly browned on all sides, then transfer to the pan with the onions.

2 Pour the wine into the frying pan, reduce by half, then pour into the saucepan. Add the chorizo, morcilla, ham bone, and bay leaf to the saucepan, season to taste, then pour in enough cold water to cover.

3 Bring to a boil, reduce the heat, cover, and simmer for around 1 hour 30 minutes. Add the potatoes and carrots, and continue to cook for 30 minutes. Add the chickpeas and cabbage, and cook for 15 minutes more.

4 To serve, remove the bay leaf and ham bone, and divide the meat and vegetables between warmed plates. Add a few spoonfuls of the hot broth, and sprinkle with parsley.

Morcilla de Burgos
This well-spiced Spanish blood sausage with rice keeps its texture and holds up to punchy flavors.

Swedish sausage casserole

When the weather turns cold, you'll find this thick, winter stew is a simple, pleasing dish. The sausages are poached in the stock, giving them a rather pale appearance and soft texture. For a complete one-pot supper, just add frozen peas for the last five minutes, and stir in a good spoonful of whole-grain mustard.

SERVES 4

PREP 10 MINS

COOK 35–45 MINS

SPECIAL EQUIPMENT LARGE CAST-IRON CASSEROLE

INGREDIENTS

2 tbsp light olive oil

2 tbsp unsalted butter

1 onion, roughly chopped

1 leek, white part only, trimmed and chopped

1½ tbsp all-purpose flour

1 quart hot chicken or beef stock

1lb 2oz (500g) waxy or semi-waxy potatoes, peeled and cut into 1in (3cm) chunks

9oz (250g) carrots, cut into ½in (1cm) rounds

8 good-quality fresh pork sausages

1 bay leaf

1 bouquet garni

salt and freshly ground black pepper

SAUSAGE ALTERNATIVES
- Salsicce fresche
- Breakfast sausage
- Boerewors

1 In a large, cast-iron casserole, heat the oil and butter over medium heat. Add the onion and leek, and cook gently for 5 minutes, until softened. Sprinkle over the flour, and stir it in well. Continue to cook for a couple of minutes, to brown the flour slightly.

2 Gradually stir in the stock, and bring to a boil. It should thicken slightly as it heats. When it boils, add the potatoes and carrots.

3 Pierce the sausages with a fork, and add them to the casserole, making sure that everything is submerged.

4 Add the bay leaf and bouquet garni, and season well. Cover and cook over low heat for 20–30 minutes, until the vegetables are soft, and the sausages cooked through. The cooking time will depend on the type of potatoes. It is ready once the potatoes are cooked, but be sure not to let them fall apart. Remove the bay leaf and bouquet garni, and serve.

Lentils, spaetzle, and frankfurters

This classic German dish comes from the southern province of Swabia. The addition of vinegar here may seem unusual, but it really complements the dish. Spaetzle is a simple pasta from the region. It looks rather rustic, but tastes delicious.

SERVES 4

PREP 30 MINS

COOK 1 HR

SPECIAL EQUIPMENT SPAETZLE PAN OR PRESS (OPTIONAL)

INGREDIENTS

For the lentils and frankfurters

9oz (250g) brown lentils, washed and drained

1 bay leaf

2 tbsp olive oil

3½oz (100g) speck or Pancetta, chopped

1 onion, finely chopped

1 large carrot, finely chopped

1 celery stalk, trimmed and chopped

2 garlic cloves, crushed

2 tbsp all-purpose flour

2 cups chicken stock

salt and freshly ground black pepper

8 German Frankfurter Würstchen or Wiener Würstel

2 tbsp red wine vinegar

2 tbsp finely chopped flat-leaf parsley

For the spaetzle

3¼ cups all-purpose flour

4 large eggs

½ cup milk

¼ tsp freshly grated nutmeg

4 tbsp unsalted butter, plus extra for greasing

SAUSAGE ALTERNATIVES

• American frankfurters
• Kiełbasa czosnkowa or zwyczajna
• Parówka

1 Put the lentils in a saucepan with the bay leaf, and cover with water. Bring to a boil, then simmer for 20 minutes. Drain.

2 In a large, heavy saucepan, heat the oil. Brown the speck, then add the onion, carrot, and celery, cooking until softened. Stir in the garlic. Stir in the flour and cook for 2–3 minutes. Add the stock, lentils, and seasoning. Simmer for 10 minutes. Add the frankfurters, and stir in the vinegar and parsley.

3 Meanwhile for the spaetzle, sift the flour, and season. Beat together the eggs, milk, nutmeg, and ½ cup water. Add to the flour, and mix to form a dough.

4 Bring a large pan of salted water to a boil. Press the mixture through a lightly greased colander (with ½in (1cm) holes), or a spaetzle pan or press, into the water. Cook for 1–2 minutes. When the spaetzle rise to the top, remove with a slotted spoon.

5 Heat the butter in a frying pan. Add the spaetzle, season, and toss until brown. Serve with the lentils and frankfurters.

Choucroûte garnie

A simpler version of a classic dish from the Alsace region of France, this one-pot meal is excellent for hearty appetites on a cold night. You can prepare the recipe up to step three, cool, and refrigerate. Cook the sausages and reheat the dish the next day for a speedy meal.

SERVES 6–8

PREP 30 MINS

COOK 3 HRS

SPECIAL EQUIPMENT LARGE FLAMEPROOF CASSEROLE

INGREDIENTS

3 tbsp goose fat, or sunflower oil

9oz (250g) piece smoked ham, chopped

1lb 2oz (500g) pork spare ribs, sliced to separate

2 onions, chopped

2 green apples, cored and sliced

1 garlic clove, finely chopped

6 black peppercorns, lightly crushed

6 juniper berries, lightly crushed

large sprig of thyme

2 bay leaves

24oz (600g) jar sauerkraut, thoroughly drained and rinsed

1¼ cups light beer or Riesling wine

2 cups chicken stock

12 small new potatoes

12oz (350g) saucisse de Strasbourg

salt and freshly ground black pepper

chopped flat-leaf parsley, to serve

SAUSAGE ALTERNATIVES
• Knackwurst
• Mährische
• Montbéliard

1 Heat 2 tablespoons of goose fat in a large, flameproof casserole and cook the ham and ribs, turning, for 3–4 minutes, or until evenly colored. Remove the meat and keep warm. Add the onions to the pan and cook for 2–3 minutes.

2 Add the apples, garlic, peppercorns, juniper berries, thyme, and bay leaves. Stir in the sauerkraut, return the ham and pork, and pour in the beer (or wine) and stock. Place a piece of waxed paper on top, cover tightly with a lid, and simmer over very low heat for 2 hours.

3 Add the potatoes, pushing them down into the sauerkraut. Cover and cook over low heat for 50–60 minutes, or until tender.

4 Meanwhile, heat the remaining fat in a frying pan, and cook the sausages until brown, turning once. Spoon the sauerkraut mixture on to a large platter and arrange the sausages on top. Season to taste, sprinkle with parsley, and serve.

Saucisse de Strasbourg
This sausage shows the influence of the German border close to Strasbourg. It is simmered to eat and imparts a rich flavor to stews.

Fabada

This spicy Spanish sausage and bacon stew is ideal comfort food. This simple time-saving version uses canned beans. Omit the red wine if you prefer, and use more chicken stock instead. Serve it with a mixed salad, and plenty of crusty bread to soak up the rich juices.

SERVES 4

PREP 5 MINS

COOK 40 MINS

INGREDIENTS

9oz (250g) morcilla

9oz (250g) chorizo

9oz (250g) thick-cut bacon, tocino, or pancetta

1 tbsp olive oil

¼ cup red wine

2 x 14oz cans white beans, drained

pinch of saffron threads

1 bay leaf

2 cups chicken stock

SAUSAGE ALTERNATIVES

• Instead of morcilla:
buristo, boudin noir, or schwarzwurst

• Instead of chorizo:
American andouille, merguez, or
kiełbasa zwyczajna

1 Cut the morcilla, chorizo, and bacon into large chunks. Heat the oil in a large saucepan over medium-low heat. Add the sausages and bacon, and cook, stirring, for 2 minutes.

2 Increase the heat, add the wine, and allow it to bubble and reduce for 2–3 minutes.

3 Stir in the beans, saffron, bay leaf, and just enough stock to cover. Bring to a boil, reduce the heat, cover, and simmer for 30 minutes. Serve hot.

Chorizo Asturiano
Generously flavored with garlic, oregano, and hot paprika, this is an ideal cooking chorizo. It works well with other robust flavors.

Lamb sausage kebabs with tzatziki dip

A juicy take on lamb köfte, these will be a surefire hit at any barbecue. Outside the summer months, they can be easily broiled instead. Squeezing the liquid from the cucumber will prevent your tzatziki from becoming watery, and don't make it too far ahead either; it becomes more garlicky the longer it sits.

SERVES 4

PREP 20 MINS, PLUS 1 HR MARINATING AND 1 HR SOAKING

COOK 10 MINS

SPECIAL EQUIPMENT
8 WOODEN SKEWERS

INGREDIENTS

1 large zucchini

4 scallions, white parts only, cut in half

salt and freshly ground black pepper

2 tbsp olive oil

4 tbsp chopped mint

4in (10cm) length of cucumber, around 5½oz (150g), quartered lengthwise and seeded

¾ cup Greek yogurt

1 garlic clove, crushed

8 fresh lamb sausages

SAUSAGE ALTERNATIVES
• Fresh pork sausage
• Fresh beef sausage

1 Soak the skewers in water for 1 hour. This prevents them from burning during cooking.

2 Remove the ends of the zucchini, then, using a potato peeler, cut 16 wide strips lengthwise. Place the zucchini and scallions in a bowl and season. Add the oil and 1 tablespoon of mint and marinate for 1 hour.

3 To make the tzatziki, grate the cucumber and place in a sieve, pressing down well to remove excess liquid. Mix with the yogurt, garlic, and remaining mint, and season.

4 Put the sausages in the zucchini marinade and stir to coat. Pierce them all over with a fork. Preheat the broiler, if using.

5 Thread one end of a sausage on to a skewer. Fold a piece of zucchini in half, then in half again, and thread on to the skewer. Follow with a piece of scallion, then another piece of zucchini. Top with the other end of the sausage. Repeat to make 8 crescent-shaped kebabs.

6 Grill or broil the kebabs over low heat for 10 minutes, turning. Serve with the tzatziki, green salad, and crusty bread.

Sausage and mustard casserole

Pure winter bliss, this recipe is guaranteed to become a family favorite. Serve it with creamy mashed potatoes and lightly steamed cabbage. You can vary the types of mustards as you prefer, but the dish is especially good with whole-grain mustard, which adds consistency and complexity to the flavor.

SERVES 6

PREP 15 MINS

COOK 45 MINS

SPECIAL EQUIPMENT LARGE FLAMEPROOF CASSEROLE

INGREDIENTS

1 tbsp olive oil

12 good-quality fresh pork sausages

1 large onion, finely sliced

8oz (225g) small button mushrooms

1 cooking apple, peeled, cored, and cut into chunks

1 bay leaf

1 tbsp chopped sage

1¼ cups chicken stock

2 tsp Dijon mustard

1 tsp whole-grain mustard

1 tsp English mustard

¾ cup heavy cream

salt and freshly ground black pepper

SAUSAGE ALTERNATIVES
• Lincolnshire sausage
• Italian sausage
• Bratwurst

1 Heat the oil in a large flameproof casserole and gently cook the sausages until golden. Remove the sausages from the casserole and set aside.

2 Add the onion and cook until softened. Add the mushrooms and cook for 5 minutes, then stir in the apple, bay leaf, sage, and stock.

3 Bring to a boil, then return the sausages to the casserole. Reduce the heat, cover, and cook gently for 20 minutes, stirring often. The apple pieces should break down and thicken the sauce slightly. If they are still holding their shape, mash them with the back of a wooden spoon and stir in.

4 Mix the mustards and cream together in a bowl, and season with salt and pepper. Pour into the casserole, increase the heat, and simmer gently for 5 minutes, or until the sauce has thickened slightly. Serve.

Lincolnshire sausage
Subtly spiced, this hearty fresh sausage is best complemented by creamy mash and onion gravy.

Italian red wine and sausage stew with polenta

A fantastically simple stew with real depth of flavor. Traditionally accompanied by soft, cheesy polenta, you could also serve it with boiled new potatoes or plenty of crusty bread to soak up the rich sauce.

SERVES 4

PREP 10 MINS

COOK 1 HR

INGREDIENTS

For the sausage stew

4 tbsp olive oil

8 salsicce fresche

2 large onions, finely sliced

4 garlic cloves, finely sliced

¾ cup red wine

1½ cups chicken stock

14oz (400g) can chopped tomatoes

pinch of granulated sugar

2 tbsp finely chopped flat-leaf parsley

For the polenta

7oz (200g) instant or traditional polenta

1 quart chicken stock

2 tbsp unsalted butter

2oz (60g) Parmesan cheese, finely grated

salt and freshly ground black pepper

SAUSAGE ALTERNATIVES

• Lincolnshire sausage
• Medister pølse
• Kiełbasa biała
• Italian sausage (American)

1 Heat half the oil in a large, heavy saucepan over medium heat. Pierce the sausages, then cook until well browned. Remove and slice into chunks.

2 Add the remaining oil to the pan, and cook the onion over medium heat until well softened. Add the garlic and cook for 2–3 minutes stirring gently. Add the wine, stock, tomatoes, and sugar, and bring to a boil. Reduce the heat to a low simmer and cook, uncovered, for 30 minutes. Add the sausages and cook for 10–15 minutes, stirring occasionally, until thickened. Stir in the parsley.

3 Meanwhile, if using instant polenta, cook according to the instructions on the packet. For traditional polenta, bring the stock to a boil in a large, heavy pan. Pour in the polenta in a stream, stirring. Return to a boil, then reduce the heat to a low simmer. Cook for 40 minutes, stirring. It is ready when it comes away from the pan edges. Stir in the butter and Parmesan. Season well and serve with the stew.

Salsicce fresche
Fresh Italian pork sausage may be seasoned with a little chile, and is delicious with lentils.

Stir-fried noodles with Chinese sausage and shiitake

With its vibrant flavors that seem made for each other, this is an excellent choice for a hearty supper. The Chinese sausages are flavored with soy, and lend a deep umami flavor to a bowl of slippery rice noodles.

SERVES 4

PREP 10 MINS, PLUS
30 MINS SOAKING

COOK 15 MINS

SPECIAL EQUIPMENT WOK

INGREDIENTS

10oz (300g) flat rice noodles

2 tbsp sunflower or vegetable oil, plus extra for the noodles

¾oz (20g) dried shiitake mushrooms

2 large eggs, beaten

1 tbsp chili oil

7oz (200g) Chinese sausages, thinly sliced on the diagonal

6 scallions, trimmed, and thinly sliced on the diagonal

3 garlic cloves, finely sliced

5½oz (150g) pak choi, washed, and sliced into thin wedges

¼ cup soy sauce

2 tbsp oyster sauce

2 tbsp Chinese rice wine

pinch of granulated sugar

4 tbsp chopped cilantro

SAUSAGE ALTERNATIVES
• Dried chistorra
• Kabanos
• Linguiça

1 Soak the noodles in hot water for 30 minutes until soft, then drain, rinse, and toss with oil to stop them from sticking together. While the noodles are soaking, place the mushrooms in a bowl and cover with boiling water. Soak for 20 minutes. Drain (reserve the liquid), squeeze out excess water, then finely slice.

2 Heat 1 tablespoon of the oil in a wok until hot. Add the eggs, and stir-fry until cooked. Remove, cut into strips, and set aside. Wipe the wok clean with paper towels, if necessary.

3 Heat another tablespoon of oil, and the chili oil. Add the sausage and stir-fry until it starts to release fat. Add the scallions and garlic, and stir-fry for an additional minute. Add the pak choi and mushrooms with ¼ cup of the reserved mushroom liquid, and cook for 2 minutes, until the pak choi starts to wilt.

4 Add the noodles and return the omelette strips to the wok. Pour in the soy sauce, oyster sauce, rice wine, and sugar. Cook for 2–3 minutes. Stir in the cilantro before serving.

Couscous Royale

Richly spiced, this dish makes a colorful feast. To get ahead, you can make the spiced meat stew in advance, cool, then refrigerate for up to three days, or even freeze for one month, before reheating and serving with the cooked couscous. The flavors will deepen.

SERVES 6

PREP 10 MINS

COOK 1 HR 20 MINS

SPECIAL EQUIPMENT LARGE FLAMEPROOF CASSEROLE

INGREDIENTS

2 tbsp olive oil

1lb 5oz (600g) lean lamb leg, cut into chunks

6 chicken drumsticks and thighs

1 large red onion, sliced

2 garlic cloves, finely chopped

1 red pepper, seeded and chopped

1 eggplant, chopped

4 tsp harissa paste

1 tbsp paprika

1 tsp ground turmeric

2 zucchini, sliced

¾ cup chicken stock

14oz (400g) can chickpeas, drained

14oz (400g) can chopped tomatoes

6oz (175g) cooked merguez, thickly sliced

salt and freshly ground black pepper

large sprig of thyme

1 bay leaf

1lb (450g) couscous, cooked according to packet instructions

roughly chopped cilantro, to serve

SAUSAGE ALTERNATIVES
• American andouille
• Chinese sausage
• Chouriço de porco preto

1 Heat the oil in a large flameproof casserole, and brown the lamb and chicken in batches, turning occasionally. Remove from the pan and set aside to drain on paper towels.

2 Add the onion, garlic, pepper, and eggplant, and cook, stirring for 3–4 minutes. Stir in the harissa, paprika, and turmeric, and cook for an additional minute.

3 Return the lamb and chicken to the pan, then add the zucchini, stock, chickpeas, tomatoes, and merguez, and season to taste. Bring to a boil, add the thyme and bay leaf, reduce the heat, cover tightly, and simmer gently over low heat for 1 hour, or until the meats are tender.

4 Strain off the liquid, pour it into a wide pan, and bring to a boil, until slightly reduced. Stir the meats and vegetables into the cooked couscous. Cover with the reserved liquid, and sprinkle with cilantro to serve.

Chorizo Basquais
Semi-cured and air-dried, this cooking chorizo is fabulous with rice and beans, or lentils, or in stews.

Lentil and Toulouse sausage casserole

A robust dish that will hit the spot on cold days and fill you up. When slowly cooked like this, the lentils become soft and tender and wonderfully flavored by the sausages. The punchy taste of Toulouse sausage makes a delicious companion to the comforting, herby flavor of the beans.

SERVES 4–6

PREP 15 MINS

COOK 1 HR 45 MINS

SPECIAL EQUIPMENT LARGE OVENPROOF CASSEROLE

INGREDIENTS

2 tbsp olive oil

1lb 5oz (600g) saucisse de Toulouse, roughly chopped

1 onion, finely chopped

2 carrots, finely chopped

freshly ground black pepper

3 garlic cloves, finely chopped

5oz (140g) chorizo, chopped

3 sprigs of rosemary

few sprigs of thyme

7oz (200g) Green French or brown lentils, rinsed and picked over for stones

¾ cup red wine

3 cups hot chicken stock

1 red chile, left whole

extra virgin olive oil, to serve

SAUSAGE ALTERNATIVES
• Boerewors
• Cumberland sausage
• Luganega
• Fresh chistorra

1 Preheat the oven to 325°F (160°C). Heat half the oil in a large ovenproof casserole over high heat, add the saucisse de Toulouse, and cook until they begin to turn golden. Set aside.

2 Add the remaining oil, onion, and carrots, and turn to coat. Season with pepper and cook for a few minutes, stirring occasionally. Add the garlic, chorizo, and herbs, and stir. Return the saucisse de Toulouse and stir in the lentils. Add the wine, bring to a boil, and cook for a minute.

3 Pour in the stock, bring to a boil, then reduce to a simmer. Add the chile, cover, and put in the oven for 1½ hours. Check occasionally that it is not drying out, adding a bit of hot water if needed. Taste and season, remove the chile, then ladle into warmed bowls and serve with a splash of extra virgin olive oil and crusty bread.

Saucisse de Toulouse
This coiled sausage with pepper is a great addition to cassoulet, or any stew with beans.

Jambalaya

This one-pot meal captures the authentic Creole and cajun flavors of Louisiana. Leave the seeds in the very hot Scotch bonnet chile if you dare! Enjoy with rustic bread to soak up the juices.

SERVES 4–6

PREP 30 MINS

COOK 45 MINS

SPECIAL EQUIPMENT LARGE HEAVY-BOTTOMED POT OR DUTCH OVEN

INGREDIENTS

¼ cup bacon dripping,s or ¼ cup vegetable or sunflower oil

4 skinless, boneless chicken thighs, cut into bite-sized pieces

8oz (225g) mix of garlic and spicy sausages (smoked if desired), cut into thick slices

1 onion, finely chopped

2 garlic cloves, finely chopped

1 red and 1 green bell pepper, seeded, and finely chopped

1 celery stalk, thinly sliced

1 Scotch bonnet chile, seeded, and finely chopped

12oz (350g) long-grain rice

1 tsp chili powder

1 tsp Worcestershire sauce

2 tbsp tomato paste

2 bay leaves

2 tsp dried thyme

1 tsp salt

½ tsp smoked paprika

pinch of sugar

freshly ground black pepper

14oz (400g) can chopped tomatoes

2 cups chicken or vegetable stock, or water

12 large raw shrimp, heads and tails removed, and deveined

1 Melt half the drippings or oil in a large heavy-bottomed pot or Dutch oven over high heat. Add the chicken and cook until browned and the juices run clear. Remove and set aside on paper towels.

2 Heat the remaining drippings or oil in the pot. Add the sausages, but not smoked sausages (if using), and cook, stirring, until browned. Remove and set aside with the chicken.

3 Reduce the heat to medium, then add the onion, garlic, bell peppers, celery, and chile, and cook for 5 minutes. Add the rice and chili powder, and cook, stirring, for 1–2 minutes. Add the Worcestershire sauce and tomato paste, and cook, stirring for another minute.

4 Return the chicken, sausages, including smoked (if using), bay leaves, thyme, salt, paprika, and sugar, and season. Pour in the tomatoes and stock, and bring to a boil, stirring. Reduce the heat to low, cover, and simmer for 12–15 minutes.

5 Add the shrimp, cover, and simmer for 3–5 minutes, or until they are pink. Serve with hot pepper sauce and rustic bread.

Spicy clam and sausage stew

Based on the classic Portuguese stew Cataplana, this tasty dish is sometimes cooked with the addition of cubed pork shoulder. Find a good fishmonger for the clams, and check them carefully to make sure they are all fresh.

SERVES 4

PREP 20 MINS,
PLUS OVERNIGHT SOAKING

COOK 1 HR 20 MINS–1 HR 30 MINS

INGREDIENTS

3½oz (100g) dried chickpeas,
soaked overnight in cold water

1lb 2oz (500g) clams

1–2 tbsp olive oil

1 large onion, finely chopped

4 garlic cloves, roughly chopped

1lb 2oz (500g) fresh chouriço,
skinned, and roughly chopped
in ½in (1cm) pieces

3½oz (100g) pancetta,
finely chopped

1 tsp smoked paprika

2 dried red chiles, finely chopped,
seeded, if you prefer

1¼ cups fish stock

14oz (400g) can chopped tomatoes

¾ cup white wine

1 bay leaf

4 tbsp roughly chopped
flat-leaf parsley

salt and freshly ground black pepper

SAUSAGE ALTERNATIVES
• Chorizo Riojano
• Merguez
• Kiełbasa wiejska

1 Drain and rinse the chickpeas. Cover with water and bring to a boil. Reduce the heat and simmer for 30 minutes until cooked, but still al dente. Drain and set aside.

2 Wash the clams in water, discarding any that are open, and do not close when tapped against the work surface.

3 Heat the oil in a large, heavy saucepan. Add the onion, and cook over medium heat for 5 minutes, until softened. Add the garlic and cook for 2–3 minutes; it should not brown. Add the chouriço and pancetta, and brown on all sides.

4 Add the paprika, chiles, stock, tomatoes, wine, bay leaf, and chickpeas to the pot, and stir. Then add half the parsley, season, and bring to a boil. Reduce the heat to a simmer, and cook, uncovered, for 30–40 minutes, stirring occasionally.

5 Increase the heat, and stir in the clams. Cover and cook over medium-high heat until they open. Discard any that remain shut. Scatter the remaining parsley, remove the bay leaf, and serve with crusty bread.

Caldo verde

This flavorsome Portuguese soup is thickened with potatoes and makes a perfect dish for the colder months. It is also fairly healthy, and filled with greens. The quantity of sausage may seem small, but it provides the perfect amount of piquancy and substance to the soup.

SERVES 4

PREP 10 MINS

COOK 35 MINS

INGREDIENTS

5 tbsp olive oil

1 onion, finely chopped

3 garlic cloves, crushed

5½oz (150g) linguiça (about 3), skinned and finely diced

1¾lb (800g) potatoes, peeled, halved, and finely sliced

1 quart good-quality chicken stock

salt and freshly ground black pepper

7oz (200g) dark green cabbage leaves, cavolo nero, or curly kale, washed and shredded

¼ tsp smoked paprika

SAUSAGE ALTERNATIVES
• Csabai kolbász PGI
• Chorizo Asturiano
• Merguez

1 In a large, heavy saucepan, heat 4 tablespoons of the oil. Add the onion and cook over medium heat for 5 minutes, until softened. Add the garlic and linguiça and cook for 2–3 minutes, until the sausage releases its oil. Stir in the potatoes.

2 Add the stock and bring to a boil. Season with pepper and a little salt if necessary, reduce the heat, cover, and simmer for 20 minutes. The potatoes should be breaking up.

3 Blanch the cabbage in boiling salted water for 1–2 minutes, until softened. Drain and rinse in cold water. Mash the potatoes into the soup until it is smooth and thick. Add the cabbage and cook for 5 minutes.

4 Heat the remaining oil in a small saucepan. Take from the heat and stir in the paprika. Serve the soup in warmed bowls with a swirl of the spicy paprika oil on top, and plenty of crusty bread.

Linguiça
A well-spiced, cured, and smoked sausage that is a great addition to a stew.

Bigos

Considered the Polish national dish by many, bigos, or "hunter's stew," is a classic country dish. It contains a little of everything—fresh, dried, smoked, and pickled. Traditionally it was kept on the stove and added to night after night.

SERVES 6–8

PREP 30 MINS

COOK 3 HRS 30 MINS

SPECIAL EQUIPMENT LARGE FLAMEPROOF CASSEROLE

INGREDIENTS

scant 1oz (25g) dried wild mushrooms

3 tbsp olive oil

7oz (200g) boczek (Polish smoked pork belly) or thick-cut bacon, in ½in (1cm) cubes

1lb 2oz (500g) pork shoulder, in 1in (3cm) cubes

9oz (250g) cured, smoked Polish sausage, such as Kiełbasa Czosnkowa, cut into chunks

1 onion, halved and finely sliced

1 celery stalk, trimmed and sliced

1 large carrot, halved and sliced

1 leek, white part only, finely sliced

7oz (200g) white cabbage, sliced

5½oz (150g) crimini or button mushrooms

½ tsp caraway seeds

½ tsp juniper berries, roughly ground

1 tsp paprika and 1 bay leaf

1 large sprig of thyme

1 heaping tbsp all-purpose flour

salt and freshly ground black pepper

1¼ cups red wine

1½ cups chicken or beef stock

9oz (250g) sauerkraut, drained and rinsed

2 tbsp red currant jelly

1 bouquet garni

1 Soak the dried mushrooms in 2 cups of boiling water. In a large, flameproof casserole, heat 1 tablespoon oil over high heat. Add all the meat and brown on all sides. Remove from the casserole and set aside.

2 Heat an additional tablespoon of oil over medium heat. Cook the onion, celery, carrot, leek, and cabbage for 10 minutes, until softened. Remove from the casserole.

3 Heat the remaining oil over low heat, and cook the crimini or button mushrooms for 2–3 minutes. Return the meat and vegetables to the casserole, add the caraway, juniper, paprika, bay leaf, thyme, and flour, and season well. Stir over medium heat for 2–3 minutes.

4 Stir in the dried mushrooms, the soaking water, wine, and stock. Add the sauerkraut, red currant jelly, and bouquet garni, and bring to a boil. Reduce the heat to the lowest possible setting, cover, and cook for 2 hours.

5 Remove the lid and cook for a further 1 hour, until the meat is almost falling apart. Remove the bay leaf, thyme, and bouquet garni. Serve with bread or boiled potatoes.

Kiełbasa czosnkowa
Majoram and lots of garlic are the dominant flavors in this Polish sausage. Grill, use for sandwiches, or add to scrambled eggs.

Pasta with sausage and artichoke

Using good-quality pork sausages will make all the difference to the finished dish, so buy the best you can afford. Once you have mastered the recipe, you can try adding sun-dried tomatoes and capers instead of the fresh tomatoes and olives.

SERVES 4

PREP 10 MINS

COOK 20 MINS

INGREDIENTS

1 tbsp olive oil

1 onion, finely chopped

salt and freshly ground black pepper

1 fresh medium-hot red chile, seeded and finely chopped

1lb (450g) good-quality luganega, skinned and chopped

pinch of dried oregano

14oz (400g) jar or can artichoke hearts, drained and roughly chopped

3 tomatoes, peeled and chopped

handful of pitted black olives

12oz (350g) penne

SAUSAGE ALTERNATIVES
• Any good-quality fresh pork sausage, such as Lincolnshire
• Bratwurst
• Saucisse de Toulouse

1 Heat the oil in a large frying pan, add the onion and a pinch of salt, and cook over low heat for 5 minutes, or until soft and translucent. Add the chile and cook for a few seconds more, then add the sausages, breaking them up with the back of a fork until they are roughly mashed.

2 Cook until the sausages are no longer pink, for about 10 minutes, stirring occasionally, then add the oregano and artichokes and cook for a few minutes more. Stir in the tomatoes and olives, then season well.

3 Meanwhile, cook the pasta in a large pan of boiling salted water for 10 minutes, or until it is cooked but still al dente. Drain, keeping back a tiny amount of the cooking water. Return the pasta to the pan and toss together with the reserved cooking water. Combine with the sausage mixture and serve.

Luganega
This sweetly spiced, coiled Italian sausage is wonderful with a plain risotto, or with polenta.

Huevos rancheros with chorizo

This classic Mexican dish of "ranch-style eggs" makes a substantial and delicious breakfast with a fabulous chile kick. If you prepare the recipe up to the end of step three the night before, you can get it ready to serve in just five minutes.

SERVES 4

PREP 20 MINS

COOK 50 MINS

INGREDIENTS

6 tbsp olive oil

1 onion, finely chopped

2 garlic cloves, crushed

2 dried chiles, finely chopped

1 scant tsp smoked paprika

14oz (400g) can chopped tomatoes

½ tsp granulated sugar

1 tbsp chopped flat-leaf parsley

sea salt and freshly ground black pepper

10oz (300g) cooked waxy potatoes, cut into ¾in (2cm) cubes

7oz (200g) spicy Mexican chorizo, peeled if necessary, cut into ¾in (2cm) cubes

4 large eggs

2 tbsp chopped cilantro

SAUSAGE ALTERNATIVES

• Merguez
• Chistorra
• Csabai kolbász PGI

1 Heat 4 tablespoons of the oil in a small, heavy saucepan. Add the onion and cook over medium heat for 5 minutes until softened. Add the garlic, chiles, and paprika, and cook gently for 1 minute. Add the tomatoes, sugar, and parsley, and bring to a boil. Season, reduce the heat, and simmer for 30 minutes.

2 When the salsa has reduced to a thick, dark sauce, remove from the heat and mash it with a potato masher. Set aside.

3 In a large, heavy frying pan, heat the remaining oil. Cook the potatoes for 5 minutes over medium heat. Add the chorizo and cook for 5 more minutes, until everything is well browned.

4 Take the pan from the heat and stir in the tomato salsa. Make 4 large holes in the mixture and crack the eggs into the holes.

5 Return the pan to the heat and cook the eggs for 5 minutes, or until cooked as you prefer. Sprinkle with the cilantro and serve from the pan, with tortillas or crusty bread on the side.

Spetzofai

This is a rustic country stew loved all over Greece. It can be cooked using fresh or cured sausages, but choose a sausage with a rough texture for an authentic result. Many recipes add eggplant or zucchini to the list of vegetables included.

SERVES 4

PREP 20–25 MINS

COOK 55 MINS

SPECIAL EQUIPMENT
LARGE CAST-IRON CASSEROLE

INGREDIENTS

2 tbsp olive oil

1 red onion, roughly chopped

1 red bell pepper, seeded
and roughly chopped

1 green bell pepper, seeded
and roughly chopped

14oz (400g) country sausage,
such as Horiatiko, cut into
½in (1cm) chunks

1 red chile or jalapeño, seeded if
preferred, and finely chopped

2 garlic cloves, roughly chopped

1 tsp smoked paprika

4 ripe tomatoes,
peeled and puréed

7fl oz (200ml) white wine

1 heaping tbsp tomato paste

1 heaping tbsp chopped oregano

salt and freshly ground black pepper

SAUSAGE ALTERNATIVES
• Pork and leek sausage
• Salsicce fresche
• Kiełbasa biała

1 Heat the oil over medium heat in a large cast-iron casserole. Add the onion and peppers, and cook for 5 minutes, until starting to brown in places. Add the sausage, and cook over high heat for 3–5 minutes, until it is well sealed. Pour in the chile and garlic, and cook for 2–3 minutes more.

2 Add the paprika, tomatoes, wine, tomato paste, and oregano, and season well. Bring the stew to a boil, then reduce the heat to a gentle simmer and cook, covered, for 30 minutes. The vegetables should be soft, and the sausage cooked through.

3 Remove the lid and simmer for a further 5 minutes, to reduce the sauce. Serve as a starter, main course, or part of a meze-style meal.

Cassoulet

A substantial bean and meat stew from southwest France, this is a dish for a special occasion. In the winter, there is no better way to celebrate than with a table full of guests with hearty appetites, and an enormous, satisfying cassoulet.

SERVES 4–6

PREP 30 MINS, PLUS SOAKING

COOK 3 HRS 45 MINS

SPECIAL EQUIPMENT 3 QUART OVENPROOF CASSEROLE

INGREDIENTS

12oz (350g) dried haricot beans, white cannelini, or navy beans

1 tbsp olive oil

1lb 5oz (600g) saucisse de Toulouse

9oz (250g) bacon cut into small pieces

2 onions, finely chopped

1 carrot, chopped

4 garlic cloves, crushed

4 duck legs

1 sprig of thyme, plus ½ tbsp chopped leaves

1 bay leaf

salt and freshly ground black pepper

2 tbsp tomato paste

14oz (400g) can chopped tomatoes

¾ cup white wine

1 baguette (about ½ a day old)

1 tbsp chopped flat-leaf parsley

SAUSAGE ALTERNATIVES
• Any good-quality fresh pork sausage, such as Lincolnshire or Cumberland
• Bratwurst
• Luganega

1 Place the beans in a pan, cover with cold water, and boil for 10 minutes. Remove from the heat and soak for 2–3 hours, then drain.

2 Heat the oil in a frying pan and brown the sausages. Set aside. Add the bacon, cook for 5 minutes, and set aside. Add the onions and carrot, reduce the heat, and cook gently for 10 minutes. Stir in three-quarters of the garlic. Remove from the heat.

3 Preheat the oven to 425°F (220°C). Roast the duck legs for 30 minutes. Reserve their fat, and reduce the oven temperature to 275°F (140°C).

4 Place half the beans in an ovenproof casserole, then add the onions, carrot, sausages, bacon, and duck. Top with the remaining beans. Add the sprig of thyme and bay leaf, and season well.

5 Mix 3 cups hot water with the tomato paste, chopped tomatoes, and wine, then pour in to the casserole. Cover with a lid, and cook in the oven for 3 hours.

6 Process the baguette and remaining garlic into coarse crumbs. Heat 2 tablespoons of the duck fat in a frying pan and fry the crumbs until golden. Drain on paper towels and stir in the parsley and thyme leaves. Sprinkle the bread crumbs over the cassoulet, and serve.

Dirty rice

A Cajun dish from the Deep South, this gets its name from the traditional use of chicken gizzards, which were added to the rice to give the distinctive "dirty" appearance. Here they are replaced by chicken livers, which give a rich flavor as well as the classic color.

SERVES 4–6

PREP 15 MINS

COOK 1 HR
PLUS 5 MINS RESTING

SPECIAL EQUIPMENT LARGE CAST-IRON CASSEROLE

INGREDIENTS

4 tbsp olive oil

1 onion, finely chopped

1 celery stalk, trimmed, and finely sliced

1 red bell pepper, seeded and cut into ½in (1cm) cubes

1 green bell pepper, seeded and cut into ½in (1cm) cubes

14oz (400g) pork sausage

7oz (200g) chicken livers, cleaned, trimmed, and finely chopped

1 red or jalapeño chile, seeded and finely chopped

2 garlic cloves, finely chopped

1 tsp smoked paprika

1 tsp coriander seeds, crushed

10oz (300g) long-grain rice

salt and freshly ground black pepper

2½ cups hot chicken stock

leaves from 1 large sprig of thyme

handful of flat-leaf parsley, finely chopped

1 tbsp finely chopped oregano

SAUSAGE ALTERNATIVES
• Fresh poultry sausage
• Fresh beef sausage
• Bratwurst

1 Preheat the oven to 325°F (160°C). Heat 3 tablespoons of oil in a large cast-iron casserole, and add the onion, celery, and peppers. Cook over low heat for 5–7 minutes, until softened. Set aside.

2 Add the remaining oil to the casserole, then the sausage and chicken livers. Increase the heat and cook for 5 minutes, until the sausage has broken up, seared, and is no longer pink.

3 Add the chile, garlic, paprika, and coriander seeds, and cook for 2–3 more minutes. Return the vegetables to the casserole, then stir in the rice. Season well, and add the stock.

4 Bring to a boil, cover, and transfer to the oven. Cook for up to 40 minutes, stirring once or twice, until the rice is cooked and the stock has been absorbed. Remove from the oven and rest for 5 minutes. Stir in the herbs, check the seasoning, and serve with a mixed leaf salad, and crusty bread.

Claypot rice with Chinese sausage and vegetables

This fragrant, wholesome one-pot dish takes only minutes to prepare and cook. Chinese dried sausages are quite greasy, so plunging them into boiling water for a minute helps remove a little of the fat.

SERVES 4

PREP 10 MINS

COOK 20 MINS,
PLUS 5 MINS RESTING

INGREDIENTS

12oz (350g) long-grain rice, such as jasmine rice

7oz (200g) Chinese pork sausage

1 tbsp sunflower or vegetable oil

1 tsp chili oil

1 onion, finely chopped

2 garlic cloves, finely chopped

2in (5cm) piece fresh ginger, peeled, and finely chopped

5½oz (150g) broccoli rabe (trimmed weight), thicker stems halved lengthwise

5½oz (150g) asparagus (trimmed weight), thicker stems halved lengthwise

2 tbsp soy sauce

SAUSAGE ALTERNATIVES
- Chistorra
- Pepperoni
- Hauswürstel, e.g. Kärtner Hauswürstel

1 Wash the rice under running water. Plunge the sausages into a large saucepan of boiling water and cook for 1 minute. Remove the sausages from the water, allow to cool, then cut into ½in (1cm) diagonal slices.

2 In a medium-large, heavy saucepan, heat the sunflower and chili oils over low heat. Add the onion, garlic, and ginger, and cook gently until softened. Add the rice and stir, so each grain is covered with oil. Add 3 cups water. The water should come to about ¾in (2cm) above the rice.

3 Cover and bring to a boil. Reduce the heat to the lowest setting and cook for 5 minutes, until the level of the water is below that of the rice. Place the sausages on top, then the green vegetables, spreading them out evenly. Cover, and cook for 5 minutes, until the water has evaporated.

4 Turn off the heat and leave covered for a final 5 minutes. Serve from the pan, drizzled with soy sauce.

Cajun andouille gumbo

Make sure you buy a smoky Cajun-style andouille sausage for this hearty southern dish rather than the French andouille, which is made mostly from the intestines and stomach of the pig. Leave the seeds in the chile for a spicy kick, or omit them for a milder result.

SERVES 6

PREP 15 MINS

COOK 1 HR

INGREDIENTS

2 tbsp olive oil

1 large onion, finely chopped

1 green bell pepper, seeded and cut into ¾in (2cm) cubes

2 garlic cloves, crushed

2 tbsp unsalted butter

3 tbsp all-purpose flour

2 x 14oz cans chopped tomatoes

2 cups fish or chicken stock

2 dried red chiles, finely chopped

1 tsp smoked paprika

7oz (200g) okra, cleaned, trimmed, and cut into ¾in (2cm) chunks

9oz (250g) andouille smoked sausage, peeled and cut into ¾in (2cm) chunks

salt and freshly ground black pepper

1 tbsp thyme leaves

1lb 2oz (500g) large raw shrimp, peeled and deveined

2 tbsp finely chopped flat-leaf parsley

SAUSAGE ALTERNATIVES
• Smoked chorizo
• Merguez
• Kiełbasa zwyczajna

1 Heat the oil in a large, heavy saucepan. Add the onion and green pepper, and cook gently for 5 minutes until soft, but not brown. Add the garlic, and continue to cook for 2 more minutes.

2 Add the butter to the pan and allow it to melt, then add the flour and stir on very low heat for around 10 minutes, until browned. Add the tomatoes, stock, chiles, paprika, okra, and sausage, and bring to a boil. Taste and season with pepper, and salt if necessary (the stock may be salty).

3 Reduce the heat to a low simmer and add the thyme. Cook, covered, for 30 minutes, stirring occasionally, until the okra is soft and the gumbo well thickened.

4 Increase the heat and add the shrimp. Continue to cook the gumbo, uncovered, for 5 more minutes, until the shrimp are opaque and cooked through. Stir through the parsley, and serve with rice.

American andouille
Highly seasoned and smoked, this sausage spices up gumbos and jambalayas to perfection.

Black pudding with apple

Sweet apples are the perfect partner for bacon and savory, peppery British-style blood sausage. Serve this dish for breakfast or a hearty cold-weather brunch. This recipe is especially good with an apple-based chutney and whole-grain toast. For a more substantial meal, serve with creamy mashed potatoes.

SERVES 4

PREP 10 MINS

COOK 20 MINS

INGREDIENTS

3 sweet eating apples, peeled, cored, and sliced

2 tbsp unsalted butter

2 tsp light brown sugar

vegetable oil, for frying

8 large slices or 16 small slices of blood sausage, such as English or Scottish black pudding

4 smoked thick-cut bacon slices, cut lengthwise into thin strips

½ cup cider

SAUSAGE ALTERNATIVES
• Boudin noir
• Morcela
• Schwarzwurst
• Buristo

1 Cut each apple slice in half. Melt the butter in a small frying pan, add the apple pieces and sugar, and cook over medium heat, stirring frequently, for 8–10 minutes, or until softened and slightly caramelized. Remove from the heat and set aside.

2 Wipe out the pan, smear with oil, and fry the blood sausage, in batches, over medium-high heat for about 3 minutes on each side, or until slightly crisp. Remove from the pan and keep warm. Fry the bacon strips for 3 minutes, or until slightly crisp, stirring frequently. Remove from the pan, increase the heat, and pour in the cider. Allow to bubble until well reduced and syrupy, stirring to incorporate any bits stuck to the bottom of the pan.

3 Place a slice of blood sausage on each warmed plate, add a layer of apple, then continue layering with the remaining blood sausage and apple, dividing equally among the 4 portions. Top each stack with the bacon and drizzle with the pan juices.

Black Pudding (English)
Chunks of fat and subtle spicing make for a rustic texture. Excellent in a full English breakfast.

Spanish pilaf with chistorra and shrimp

Having a few types of preserved sausages means you can turn one or two ingredients from the refrigerator into this last-minute meal. Don't worry if you don't have saffron, as the chistorra will color the rice.

SERVES 4

PREP 15 MINS

COOK 20 MINS

SPECIAL EQUIPMENT WOK (OPTIONAL)

INGREDIENTS

4 tbsp olive oil

1 onion, finely chopped

½ red bell pepper, seeded and finely chopped

½ yellow bell pepper, seeded and finely chopped

7oz (200g) chistorra, cut into ½in (1cm) slices

2 large garlic cloves, finely chopped

½–1 tsp smoked paprika, to taste

1lb 5oz (600g) cooked long-grain rice (about 10oz (280g) before cooking)

1 pinch saffron threads, soaked in 1 tbsp hot water (optional)

3½oz (100g) cooked shrimp, peeled

3oz (85g) frozen peas

2 tbsp roughly chopped flat-leaf parsley

salt and freshly ground black pepper

SAUSAGE ALTERNATIVES
• Pepperoni
• Merguez
• Chorizo Basquais

1 In a wok or large frying pan, heat the oil. Add the onion and bell peppers, and cook over medium heat for 5–7 minutes, until they soften and start to brown slightly.

2 Add the chistorra and cook for 2–3 minutes more, until it releases its oil. Stir in the garlic and paprika and cook for another minute.

3 Stir in the rice, turning it through the oil so every grain is well coated. Add the soaked saffron (if using), and its water, stirring well. Continue to cook over medium heat for 3–5 minutes.

4 Add the shrimp, peas, and parsley and cook for a final 2–3 minutes, until the shrimp and peas are heated through. Season to taste, and serve with a green salad.

Chistorra
Paprika makes this thin Spanish sausage spicy.
Try it—finely diced and sautéed—with clams.

Grilled merguez with ratatouille

You may well find this Mediterranean spicy sausage dish addictive. It is important to set aside the browned vegetables separately, as they are cooked in layers later. Try to turn them over in step three in one piece; if this seems unlikely, leave them alone. They will still taste fantastic.

SERVES 4

PREP 15 MINS

COOK 50 MINS–1 HR

INGREDIENTS

8 tbsp olive oil

1 large or 2 small red bell peppers, seeded and cut into ½in (1cm) strips

2 zucchini, cut into ½in (1cm) slices

1 large white onion, cut into ½in (1cm) slices

2 large ripe tomatoes, each cut into 8 wedges

1 large eggplant, trimmed and cut into ½in (1cm) slices

2 large garlic cloves, finely chopped

2 tbsp finely chopped flat-leaf parsley

salt and freshly ground black pepper

8–12 merguez sausages, or enough to serve 4

SAUSAGE ALTERNATIVES

• American andouille
• Chorizo Mexicano
• Salsiccia di Calabria
• Chistorra

1 To make the ratatouille, heat 4 tablespoons of the oil in a large, heavy frying pan over medium heat. Separately cook the peppers, then zucchini, then the onion and tomatoes together, and lastly the eggplant, until browned. Set each aside separately.

2 Remove the pan from the heat. Place in the pan a layer of eggplant, then a layer of zucchini, then the bell peppers, then scatter over the garlic and parsley, and season well. Top with the tomato and onion mixture, and press everything down with a heatproof plate.

3 Return the pan to a low heat and cook for 30 minutes, until the vegetables are soft. Remove the plate using an oven mitt. Turn the vegetables gently with a spatula, and cook for 10 minutes over high heat until any liquid has evaporated. Set aside.

4 Pierce the merguez and broil, fry, or grill until well cooked and browned all over. Serve with the ratatouille, warm or at room temperature, and some crusty bread.

French merguez
A characteristic kick makes this North African-style sausage perfect for grilling and serving with bland starches.

Pretzel dogs

These pretzel dogs are guaranteed to be a huge hit at children's parties and are simple to prepare. They would make a great barbecue treat, too. Even if you've never tried to make a yeasted dough before, you will find this recipe is easy to use and it will become a family classic.

MAKES 8

PREP 30 MINS, PLUS 1 HR 30 MINS–2 HRS 30 MINS PROVING

COOK 15 MINS

INGREDIENTS

1 cup strong white bread flour, plus extra for dusting

¾ cup all-purpose flour

½ tsp salt

1 tbsp granulated sugar

1 tsp dried yeast

½ tbsp sunflower or vegetable oil, plus extra for greasing

8 hot dogs

mustard (optional)

For the glaze

1 tbsp baking soda

coarse sea salt

SAUSAGE ALTERNATIVES

• Saucisse de Strasbourg
• Regensburger

1 Put the flours, salt, and sugar into a bowl. In another bowl or jug, sprinkle the yeast over ⅔ cup warm water. Stir until dissolved, then add the oil.

2 Stir the liquid into the flour. Knead for 10 minutes on a floured surface until pliable. Put in a lightly oiled bowl, cover loosely with plastic wrap, and leave in a warm place for 1–2 hours, until nearly doubled in size.

3 Turn the dough on to a floured surface and knock it back to its original size. Divide into 8 equal pieces. Roll each piece into a log that is 18in (45cm) in length. Brush each hot dog with mustard, if using. Wrap the dough around in a spiral, pinching together at the top and bottom.

4 Place on lined baking sheets, cover with oiled plastic wrap and a dish towel, and leave in a warm place for about 30 minutes until well puffed up. Preheat the oven to 400°F (200°C).

5 In a large saucepan, dissolve the baking soda in 1 quart of boiling water. Poach the wrapped hot dogs for 1 minute. Dry briefly, and return to the baking sheets. Scatter with coarse salt and bake for 15 minutes.

Pizza with sausage

This recipe is incredibly versatile. For an authentic Italian taste, replace the pork sausages with the same amount of spicy, or fennel-flavored, salsicce fresche. You can also add mozzarella instead of Parmesan cheese, if you prefer, and a scattering of herbs, or even arugula, when the pizzas come out of the oven.

MAKES 4

PREP 30 MINS,
PLUS 30–40 MINS PROVING

COOK 20 MINS

INGREDIENTS

For the dough

1lb 2oz (500g) bread flour, plus extra for dusting

pinch of salt

¼oz (7g) packet dried yeast

¼ cup olive oil,
plus extra for greasing

For the topping

12 good-quality fresh pork sausages,

3½oz (100g) freshly grated Parmesan cheese (optional)

salt and freshly ground black pepper

semolina, for sprinkling

12–16 tomatoes, finely sliced

SAUSAGE ALTERNATIVES

- Salsicce fresche
- Chistorra
- Kiełbasa biała
- Merguez

1 Sift the flour and salt into a bowl and add the yeast. Slowly stir in 1½ cups warm water, then mix in the oil.

2 Place on a floured surface and knead for 10 minutes, until soft and spongy. Put in a bowl, cover with plastic wrap, and leave in a warm place for 30–40 minutes, until doubled in size.

3 Turn the dough out on to a floured surface and knock out the air. Divide into 4 pieces and roll each piece out to about 10in (25cm) in diameter.

4 Preheat the oven to its highest setting. Lightly oil four baking sheets and put them in the oven.

5 Remove the sausage from the casing, place in a dry frying pan, and cook over medium heat for 5 minutes, mashing it until crumbly and no longer pink. Stir in the Parmesan cheese (if using), and season.

6 Sprinkle the hot baking sheets with semolina and slide on the pizza bases. Cover them with tomato slices and bake for 5 minutes, then spoon the sausage on top. Bake for 10 more minutes, then serve.

Boudin noir with split pea purée

Boudin noir is a French blood sausage with a rich flavor, which is complemented here by a creamy pea purée. The purée thickens as it cools, so if you reheat it you may need to add water to loosen it.

SERVES 4

PREP 10 MINS

COOK 50 MINS

INGREDIENTS

3 tbsp olive oil

1 onion, finely chopped

2 garlic cloves, finely chopped

10oz (300g) yellow split peas, washed, and drained

1 bay leaf

1⅔ cups chicken stock

salt and freshly ground black pepper

4 boudin noir,
or enough for 4 servings

SAUSAGE ALTERNATIVES
• Morcilla
• Black pudding (Irish or English)
• Cacholeira preta

1 Heat 2 tablespoons of oil in a heavy saucepan over medium heat, and cook the onion for 5 minutes, until softened. Add the garlic, and cook for 2–3 minutes more.

2 Add the split peas, bay leaf, stock, and a little pepper, and bring to a boil. Reduce the heat to a very low simmer, cover, and cook for 30 minutes, stirring occasionally.

3 Remove the lid and cook for 10 minutes more, stirring frequently so the peas do not stick to the pan. They should become a rough purée. Add a little water if it seems dry.

4 Meanwhile, cut the boudin noir into ¾in (2cm) diagonal slices. Cook in the remaining oil over low heat for 5–7 minutes, turning gently, until well browned and cooked through. The sausage will remain soft.

5 Check the pea purée for seasoning, remove the bay leaf, and serve with the boudin noir and a green salad.

Boudin noir
The earthy flavor and soft texture of this sausage work well with fresh, crisp ingredients.

Weisswurst, pretzels, and sweet mustard

Weisswurst, or white sausage, is a delicate, pale Bavarian sausage usually made from pork or veal. Traditionally they are eaten for breakfast, and never after midday, so you may want to forego the classic accompaniment of cold beer!

SERVES 4 (MAKES 8 PRETZELS)

PREP 20 MINS,
PLUS 2–2 HRS 30 MINS PROVING

COOK 20 MINS

INGREDIENTS

For the pretzels

1⅓ cups bread flour

⅔ cup all-purpose flour, plus extra for dusting

½ tsp salt

½ tbsp granulated sugar

1 tsp dried yeast

½ tbsp vegetable or sunflower oil, plus extra for greasing

For the glaze

¼ tsp baking soda

coarse sea salt

1 large egg, beaten

For the sausages

8 Weisswurst, or enough for 4 servings

sweet German mustard, to serve

SAUSAGE ALTERNATIVES

• Boudin blanc
• Kiełbasa biała
• Bull blanc

1 Put the flours, salt, and sugar into a bowl. Dissolve the yeast in ⅔ cup warm water, then add the oil.

2 Stir the liquid into the flour, turn on to a lightly floured surface, and knead for 10 minutes. Put in a lightly oiled bowl, cover loosely with plastic wrap, and leave in a warm place for 1½–2 hours, until nearly doubled in size. Gently punch down the dough to its original size. Divide into 8.

3 Roll each piece into a log 18in (45cm) long. Take each end and cross them over each other to form a heart shape. Then twist the ends around each other as though they are linked arms. Bring up the ends to the center of the pretzel and secure each end to the sides so that the twist shape sits in the center. Repeat with the remaining pieces of dough.

4 Place the pretzels on a baking sheet, cover with oiled plastic wrap, and a dish towel, and leave in a warm place for 30 minutes, until puffed up. Preheat the oven to 400°F (200°C).

5 Dissolve the baking soda in 2 tablespoons of boiling water. Brush over the pretzels, then scatter with sea salt. Bake for 15 minutes. Brush with egg, and bake for 5 minutes more. Cool.

6 Put the sausages into a pan of boiling water, and turn off the heat. Leave for 10 minutes. Serve with the pretzels and mustard.

Weisswurst
Literally "white sausage," this delicate veal sausage is simmered in water and peeled before eating.

Chargrilled Sicilian sausages with lentil salad

Sicilian-style pork salsicce fresche are commonly flavored with fennel and can be found at any good Italian delicatessen. If you fancy something spicier, the same stores should also be able to supply you with a version with a little added chile. Because of their shape, the sausages keep their integrity well when cooked on a skewer.

SERVES 8

PREP 15 MINS, PLUS ADVANCE SOAKING AND 1 HR MARINATING

COOK 1 HR 15 MINS

SPECIAL EQUIPMENT 2 METAL SKEWERS

INGREDIENTS

16 Sicilian-style salsicce fresche

4 tbsp olive oil

handful of flat-leaf parsley, chopped

handful of mint leaves, finely sliced

6 basil leaves, finely sliced

3 sprigs of rosemary, leaves picked

For the lentil salad

10oz (300g) brown lentils

2 tbsp olive oil, plus 3 tbsp extra

1 small onion, finely chopped

¾ cup chicken stock

1 carrot, finely diced

2 celery stalks, peeled and diced

1 scallion, sliced diagonally

2 small fresh hot red chiles, seeded, and finely chopped

large handful of flat-leaf parsley, chopped

handful of chervil leaves, chopped

juice of ½ lemon

salt and freshly ground black pepper

SAUSAGE ALTERNATIVES
• Italian sausage (American)
• Fresh pork sausage

1 Soak the lentils for the lentil salad in advance. Pick over the lentils to remove any stones, rinse, and place them in a bowl of cold water to soak.

2 Form the sausages into a coil, and pierce with 2 metal skewers at right angles to hold it in place. Brush both sides with oil, and sprinkle with the parsley, mint, basil, and rosemary. Place in a dish, and allow to marinate in the refrigerator for 1 hour.

3 For the lentils, heat 2 tablespoons of oil in a heavy pan over low heat. Add the onion, and cook until translucent. Drain the lentils, add to the pan, and stir for 2 minutes. Pour in the stock, and bring to a boil. Reduce the heat, and simmer for 35 minutes, until the liquid is absorbed and the lentils are cooked. Let cool.

4 Meanwhile, heat a grill or broiler until hot. Lift the sausage coil from the marinade and grill or broil the sausages over medium heat for 30–35 minutes, turning once and brushing with the oil and herb marinade.

5 Put the lentils in a dish and add the vegetables, chiles, and herbs. In a bowl, whisk the remaining 3 tablespoons of oil with the lemon juice, stir into the lentils, and season well. To serve, remove the skewers from the sausages and serve with the lentils.

Swiss sausage and cheese salad

This unusual salad is a fantastic last-minute recipe if you don't seem to have much in the fridge. A few long-lasting ingredients, such as cooked sausage, pickles, and cheese, can soon be turned into a delicious light lunch or dinner dish.

SERVES 4

PREP 10 MINS

COOK 5 MINS, PLUS AT LEAST 30 MINS MARINATING

INGREDIENTS

4 tbsp vegetable or sunflower oil

3 tbsp white wine vinegar

pinch of granulated sugar

salt and freshly ground black pepper

1 small red onion, halved and finely sliced

9oz (250g) cooked or smoked sausage, such as Cervelas, skinned, sliced lengthwise, and cut into thin semicircles

7oz (200g) Emmental cheese, cut into thin strips

1¾oz (50g) dill pickles, drained and thinly sliced

2 tbsp finely chopped flat-leaf parsley

SAUSAGE ALTERNATIVES
• Kødpølse
• Bologna
• Lyoner Fleischwurst

1 In a serving bowl, whisk together the oil, vinegar, and sugar. Season well with salt and pepper. Toss the onion in this dressing, and leave it to marinate for at least 15 minutes. This will help to soften the onion, in terms of both taste and texture.

2 Add the sausage, cheese, and pickles to the bowl, and mix well to combine.

3 Sprinkle with parsley, and marinate for at least 15 minutes, and up to 1 hour, before serving with bread and a green salad.

Lyoner Fleischwurst
A sausage made from salted pork with a fine texture, this can include pistachios or red peppers.

Sausage pickles

Known as *utopenci*, or "drowned men," these pickled sausages are a Czech classic. They are traditionally served as a bar snack, with a slab of dry, dark bread and a glass of cold beer, but they also work well as a refrigerator standby or picnic dish.

MAKES 3 CUPS

PREP 15 MINS

COOK 5 MINS,
PLUS 5 DAYS MARINATING

INGREDIENTS

⅔ cup white wine vinegar

1 tsp black peppercorns

8–10 juniper berries or
allspice berries

2 bay leaves

½ tsp sea salt

1 tsp granulated sugar

9oz (250g) Spekáčky sausage,
skinned and cut into
½in (1cm) slices

1 small pickling cucumber
(about 3½oz (100g)), finely sliced

½ white onion, very finely sliced

SAUSAGE ALTERNATIVES
• Parówka
• Frankfurter Würstchen
• Hot dog

1 Sterilize a glass jar or container that can hold 3 cups. Preheat the oven to 275°F (140°C). Wash the jar and lid well in hot water, and drain upside-down. Place both in the oven for 15 minutes.

2 Meanwhile, in a small saucepan, heat the vinegar, ¾ cup water, peppercorns, juniper berries, bay leaves, salt, and sugar. Bring to a boil, and cook for 1 minute, stirring to dissolve the sugar. Remove from the heat and allow to cool.

3 Layer the sausage, cucumber, and onion in thin layers in the newly sterilized jar. When the liquid has cooled, pour it over the sausage and vegetables, including the seasonings.

4 Press the contents of the jar down so that they are fully submerged in the liquid. Seal the jar well and refrigerate for at least 5 days, before eating with fresh rye or country bread. The pickled sausage will keep for up to 2 weeks in the refrigerator.

Špekáčky
This is quite finely textured, like a Frankfurter. Bacon fat makes it a great campfire sausage.

Antipasto salad with artichokes and salami

There are some wonderful Italian salamis. For this recipe, try prosciutto-like Capocollo, ruby red Salame cacciatore, coarse-textured Salame Napoli, spicy Salsiccia di Calabria, or Finocchiona, which is flavored with fennel seeds. The artichokes in this salad perfectly complement the flavors and textures of the meats.

SERVES 4

PREP 10 MINS

INGREDIENTS

¼ cup extra virgin olive oil

1 tbsp lemon juice

½ tsp Dijon mustard

1 tbsp crème fraîche

salt and freshly ground black pepper

4½oz (125g) mixed salad leaves

2 large tomatoes, cut into thin wedges, or 5½oz (150g) cherry tomatoes, halved

2½oz (75g) black olives, pitted

1 ball fresh mozzarella, torn into bite-sized pieces

6 preserved artichoke hearts in oil, drained, and quartered

7oz (200g) mixed Italian salami

handful of basil leaves, roughly torn

SAUSAGE ALTERNATIVES
- Deutsche Salami
- Ungarische Salami
- Saucisson sec aux herbes

1 In a small bowl, whisk together the oil, lemon juice, mustard, and crème fraîche until the dressing emulsifies. Season to taste. Put the salad leaves into a large bowl and gently toss with half the dressing until they are all well coated.

2 Add the tomatoes and olives, and gently mix them through with your hands. Transfer this to a serving platter. Scatter the mozzarella pieces and artichoke hearts over the salad.

3 Take the slices of salami and gently fold them up between your fingers so that they stand up a little, in a sort of wave shape. Tuck them into the salad at intervals.

4 Scatter the torn basil leaves over the top, and drizzle with the remaining dressing. Serve with some fresh, crusty bread.

Salame cacciatore
This slim, fully dried Italian salami is great with good bread and olives as a simple starter.

Making sausages at home

Making your own sausages is immensely satisfying. However, sausage-making is a huge subject so, in this book, we offer a simple "starter version" of five types: fresh, scalded, cured, cooked, and blood sausage. All are delicious, and you'll love your new skill. Double the recipes to make sausages in bulk.

Equipment

Aside from knives and cutting boards, you'll need one or two special items. Suppliers of ingredients and equipment can be found online, as can second-hand equipment.

Large, deep plastic trays
For mixing spices into meats, and placing sausages after filling into skins. The deeper they are, the easier it is to mix well.

Coarse grinding plate

Fine grinding plate

Remove gristle if it clogs the blades

Tabletop hand grinder
You can buy hand grinders that clamp on to a table, both with coarse and fine plates. Some can be used with nozzle attachments for filling.

Protect your table with a folded cloth

Grinding plates
A coarse plate chops meat. A fine one produces tiny pieces; grinding twice gives a very smooth texture.

Filling nozzles
These are attachments for sausage-filling machines and grinders. Use different widths for the different sizes of skins. Two sizes will usually suffice.

Keep the coupling clear of meat and fat

Large bowls
A plastic bowl, that holds at least 1 gallon (4 liters). A bowl that can chip is dangerous for mixing raw meat.

Grinder attachment for food processor or mixer
You can buy grinding attachments for your existing food processor or mixer. Food processor blades are unsuitable for grinding meat.

Use a plunger, not your fingers, to feed meat into the grinder

Wash thoroughly after use, as salt corrodes metal

Electric grinder
This takes the hard work out of grinding meat and, being quicker, helps to keep the meat cool.

Large funnel
A funnel must be fairly wide. You'll need a wooden or plastic stick to push the meat down into the skins.

Sausage filler
Makes the job quicker and cleaner. Some food mixers have these as attachments.

HYGIENE AND HEALTH

CLEANLINESS
It is crucial that everything is kept both clean and cold when making sausages, especially if the sausage is to be eaten uncooked. The more meat is chopped or ground, and other ingredients added, the more high-risk a product it becomes. Wearing food-grade plastic gloves helps to prevent contamination.

STORING AND COOKING TEMPERATURES
Critical temperatures are given in the recipes but, unless otherwise stated, try to work in as cold an environment as possible, and refrigerate your sausages to below 40°F (4°C). Thorough cooking to a minimum internal temperature of 160°F (70°C) will destroy harmful bacteria. Use a meat thermometer to check the temperatures.

ROUNDWORMS
Roundworms are parasites of pigs that are destroyed by cooking, and when the meat is correctly cured or salted. Some countries are free of trichinosis but, if unsure, pork for sausages eaten raw should be frozen for a minimum of 20 days at 5°F (-15°C) if less than 6in (15cm) thick, or 30 days if thicker.

Cook in batches to prevent overcrowding

4-5 gallon boiling pan
To scald or cook sausages, a 4-5 gallon (20-liter) pan allows them to move freely, and cook evenly. Don't overcrowd the pan.

Sausage ingredients

Almost any ingredient can be used to make sausages, as you will see in this book. Using the best quality ingredients possible will produce the finest sausages, and do make sure that all spices and herbs are as fresh as they can be, because they quickly lose their aromas and flavors as they age.

Pork shoulder

Pork belly with soft fat

Dried sage

Sweet paprika

Hard back fat

Meat
Shoulder is the preferred cut for sausages; it should be very fresh. Remove excess gristle and sinew, and any blood spots. If you do not have a grinder, buy ground meat and use it immediately.

Fat
This lubricates sausages and makes them taste good. Hard back fat is used for texture and in salamis; soft belly fat melts quickly, adding succulence. If no filler is used, the usual ratio is 1:4 fat to lean meat.

Spices and herbs
Use dried herbs for enhanced flavor and measure them accurately, using one-third of the weight of fresh herbs. To check seasonings, cook a small patty and taste before filling the skins.

Curing salt
This is non-iodized salt with very small amounts of sodium nitrate or nitrite, and it reduces harmful bacteria. Always adhere to the supplier's instructions, as different salt cures are designed for specific recipes. Never use old-fashioned saltpeter as it is poisonous.

Fillers
Using fillers makes sausages soft and moist, and they allow the fat content to be adjusted. Use dried bread crumbs, oatmeal, bulgur wheat, or rice. They should be as dry as possible.

Liquid
Adding some liquid (usually iced water) helps to ease the sausage into the casings and reduces air bubbles. Wine or fruit juice add different flavors. Wine vinegar helps to ferment sausages.

Sausage skins

Also called "casings," sausage skins come in many widths. Natural skins make the best quality sausages, as they are more resilient, easier to form into links, and do not toughen when cooked. They come either dry salted or in brine and need soaking. They are sold in bundles and by length.

Hog casings

Hog casings are the most common kind of all. They are used to make chorizo, kielbasa, and the thicker types of fresh or scalded sausages.

Sheep casings

Sheep casings are more expensive, but are thin, strong, and make the most tender eating. They are used to make slim fresh sausages and Frankfurters.

Ox runners

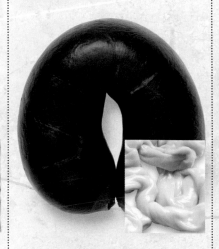

Also known as beef runners, these are used for blood sausages, ring sausages, and slim dried sausages. They are suitable for longer cooking.

Beef bungs

Also known as beef caps or ox bungs, these are used for large cooked sausages such as haggis, and many forms of dried sausage.

Collagen casings

Made from reconstituted cowhide, these casings don't need soaking but are harder to make into attractive sausages. They can toughen up while cooking.

Synthetic casings

Useful for cooked sausages, especially the thicker kinds, as there is no danger of them disintegrating while cooking. Remove before eating.

Preparing and filling skins

When making sausages for the first time, it is far easier (and more fun) to have two people: one to turn the filler handle; the other to hold the skins while they are being filled. It does get easier with practice! Don't worry if your sausages are misshapen, they will still taste delicious.

1 Soak casings overnight, or brined casings for 30 minutes, then drain. Run fresh water through them. Tie a knot at one end. Keep in cold water.

2 Open the unknotted end and slip it over the nozzle, pulling up the rest. Keep damp. Squeeze out extra air or they could burst when cooking.

3 Holding gently but firmly, push in the meat. If it bursts, break the sausage and knot the end again. For links or cooked sausages, don't overfill.

Shaping sausages

There are many traditional ways of forming the different shapes of sausages. Skilled butchers handlink sausages with dexterity, but there are easier ways of doing this at home. Always remember to use food preparation gloves while working.

Forming twisted links

1 Twist the end of the sausage to close it. Decide a size and pinch the length at that point, easing the meat away to form a gap in the casing.

2 Twist the casing twice between the sausages. Pinch the meat again to form the next sausage, but twist the casing in the opposite direction.

3 Continue along the length of the sausage. Check if any are loosely filled. Push the meat away from the twist, twisting again to tighten.

Forming coils

Small coils are easiest to make with thin sheep casings. Start the coil in the center and wind the length of sausage around to the desired width, keeping it tightly coiled. Secure with a skewer for cooking.

Forming tied links

Tie the end of the sausage firmly. Decide on the length you want, and pinch at that point. Knot 2 pieces of string—at least ½in (1cm) apart—between each sausage, so they can be cut between the strings.

Forming rings

Leave 2½in (6cm) of empty skin at the end of each sausage and remove all air. Make a knot at the end of each piece of skin. Bring the two ends together to form a ring, and tie them together.

Smoking

Home smoking is very rewarding. However, smoking does not preserve sausages, it only flavors them. Cold smoking is a lengthy process, but hot smoking is easily done at home. Sausages can be lightly smoked before being scalded or grilled, and hot smoking can cook them completely.

Tabletop smoker

Types of smokers

Smoking bags
These single-use bags have a choice of wood chips. Brush the sausages with oil and bake them in the smoking bag in a hot oven for 30–40 minutes. They emerge both smoked and cooked.

Tabletop smoker
Several models of this type of smoker are available. They are inexpensive, can be reused, and are ideal for camping. Stainless steel is the best material as it does not rust.

Larger smokers/Barbecue grill smokers
Although more expensive, some models can do cold smoking as well, and the barbecue kind can also be used for regular grilling.

205

Making a fresh sausage

This plump sausage is best suited to grilling or frying. Use sheep casings if you would prefer to make thinner sausages. Vary the spices and herbs according to taste, and omit the bread crumbs or oatmeal if you like. Wrap the sausages in plastic wrap, in convenient one- or two-portion amounts, before freezing.

MAKES 5½LB (2.5KG)

KEEPS FOR 2–3 DAYS IN THE REFRIGERATOR; FOR UP TO 4 MONTHS IN THE FREEZER

SPECIAL EQUIPMENT
LARGE 4–5 QUART (5–6 LITER) UNBREAKABLE MIXING BOWL; GRINDER; SAUSAGE FILLER; FOOD GRADE PLASTIC GLOVES

INGREDIENTS

2¾lb (1.25kg) lean pork

1lb 2oz (500g) belly pork

1lb 2oz (500g) pork back fat

3oz (85g) salt

1½ tsp dried sage

1 tsp freshly ground black pepper

1 tsp ground nutmeg

½ tsp ground ginger

6oz (180g) bread crumbs or medium oatmeal

1⅛ cups iced water

20 feet (6 meters) ¾–1½in (28–35mm) sheep or hog casings, soaked and one end knotted

SAUSAGE-MAKING TIP
If you put the fat into the freezer for 30 minutes, it will grind more easily without melting.

1 Chop the meat and fat into chunks, and chill thoroughly. Grind the meat and fat through a coarse grinding plate on to a deep, wide tray, putting alternate pieces of meat and fat through the grinder.

2 Mix the salt, herbs, and spices with the bread crumbs or oatmeal. Sprinkle this mixture over the ground meat and start to mix. Drizzle in the water and mix thoroughly to distribute the spices.

3 Test the mixture by making a small patty and cooking it in a frying pan. Taste to check if it is to your liking. If more spices are needed, add them and mix well.

4 Grind the mixture through a fine grinding plate. Fit a skin on to the filler nozzle and fill the sausages. Do not fill the skin too tight, or it will burst when making links.

5 Twist the end of the sausage to close it. Decide on the length you want each sausage to be, and pinch the length at that point, easing the sausage away to form a gap in the casing. Twist the sausage twice. When making the next sausage, always twist in the opposite direction, otherwise the links will unravel easily. If air bubbles remain, pierce the skin at that point with a sterilized needle or toothpick. If the mixture is too loose within the skin, firm it up by squeezing from the nearest link and twisting once more.

Best with...
There are so many ways to cook fresh sausages. Everybody loves them grilled—pair with oysters for a treat—or braise with beans and tomatoes.

Making a scalded sausage

There is a huge family of these popular scalded sausages, ranging in length, width, and color. Many are smoked, which gives each its characteristic color, but this delicate, herb-speckled sausage is unsmoked, similar to a bockwurst. This process gives a firm texture, which remains when the sausage is reheated on the grill or in the oven.

MAKES 6LB (2.75KG)

KEEPS FOR 2 DAYS IN THE REFRIGERATOR; FOR UP TO 4 MONTHS IN THE FREEZER

SPECIAL EQUIPMENT
GRINDER; LARGE CONTAINERS; SAUSAGE FILLER; LARGE BOILING PAN; MEAT THERMOMETER; FOOD GRADE PLASTIC GLOVES

COOK 20 MINUTES

INGREDIENTS

3lb 3oz (1.5kg) veal shoulder

1lb 10oz (750g) pork shoulder

9oz (250g) pork back fat

1 large onion, finely chopped

1½ tbsp finely chopped chives

1½ tbsp finely chopped parsley

2 tbsp salt

½ tsp ground cloves

1 tsp freshly ground white pepper

1 tsp sweet paprika

2 large eggs, beaten

1¼ cups milk

20 feet (6 meters) ¾–1½in (28–35mm) sheep or hog casings, soaked and one end knotted

> **SAUSAGE-MAKING TIP**
> Chill all meat and equipment before using, by placing it in the freezer for 30–40 minutes.

1 Chop all the meat into rough chunks, removing any sinew and gristle you find as you go along, and chill thoroughly. Grind the meat and fat alternately through a fine grinding plate, to avoid clogging the grinder.

2 Mix the onions, herbs, salt, and spices, then sprinkle them over the meat and mix thoroughly, until everything is very well and evenly blended together. Take your time and be meticulous.

3 Spread out thinly and chill in the freezer for 30–40 minutes. Grind again through a fine grinding plate. Beat the eggs with the milk, and add to the meat mixture.

4 Mix thoroughly (doing this in two batches then combining them makes it easier). Cook a small patty of the sausage, and taste. If needed, add more spices and mix well.

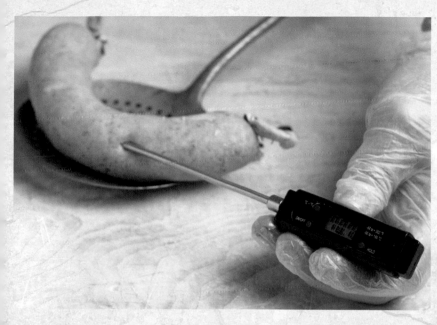

5 Fill the skins gently, and not too tightly (see page 204). Tie into links and pierce each with a sterilized needle or a toothpick. Bring a large pan of water to a boil and lower in the string of sausages (don't cut them until cooked to prevent leakage— the sausage can swell). Simmer for 20 minutes, or until the internal temperature is 160°F (70°C). Lift the sausages carefully into cold water to cool until the internal temperature is below 100°F (40°C). Rinse quickly with hot water to remove any grease, then allow them to dry off. Cover, and keep refrigerated until you are ready to cook and serve them.

Best with...
Grilled or gently simmered in broth or water, these are delicious on a toasted roll with mustard.

Making a cooked sausage

This is a sausage for cold cutting, which has a smoky flavor from the bacon. Grinding the meat twice gives it a characteristic smooth texture; for an even smoother result, start with meat that has already been finely ground. While it can be enjoyed cold, or as part of an antipasti, this sausage can also be cooked in many dishes.

MAKES 4 × 1LB 2OZ (500G) SAUSAGES

KEEPS FOR 7 DAYS IN THE REFRIGERATOR; FOR 2 DAYS ONCE CUT OPEN

SPECIAL EQUIPMENT GRINDER; LARGE CONTAINERS; SAUSAGE FILLER; LARGE BOILING PAN; MEAT THERMOMETER; FOOD GRADE PLASTIC GLOVES

COOK 1–1½ HRS, PLUS 24 HRS CURING

INGREDIENTS

1lb 2oz (500g) pork back fat

2¼lb (1kg) lean beef, coarsely chopped

9oz (250g) lean pork, coarsely chopped

9oz (250g) smoked bacon, coarsely chopped

1 tsp coarsely ground black pepper

1 tsp ground nutmeg

1 tbsp curing salt

1 garlic clove, finely chopped

1 large onion, finely chopped

⅔ cup iced water

1 tsp whole black peppercorns

4 × 12in (30cm) lengths of 4in (105mm) synthetic casing

> **SAUSAGE-MAKING TIP**
> Make your sausages short enough to fit comfortably into your boiling pan without touching the sides.

1 Put the back fat in the freezer for 30 minutes to firm it. Grind the lean meats and bacon through a fine grinding plate. Mix all the seasonings, curing salt, garlic, and onion together.

2 Stir the onion and salt mixture into the water and sprinkle it over the meats. Mix thoroughly, then grind again through a fine plate—the texture should be almost a paste.

3 Cut the back fat into ¼–½in (½–1cm) cubes and add this, with the peppercorns, to the mixture. Mix thoroughly once more. Cover and put in the refrigerator to cure for 24 hours at 40°F (4°C).

4 Tie one end of a casing tightly with butcher's string, leaving about 2in (5cm) of spare string. Stuff the sausage mixture into the open end, packing it as tightly as possible so all the air is excluded.

5 Tie securely using a special knot that won't slip off during cooking. Twist the skin to close and bind tightly with string. Then open out both ends and tie firmly into "ears" (see above).

6 Half-fill a boiling pan with water and bring to a boil. Reduce the heat to a gentle simmer and add the sausages without crowding the pan, making sure they have room to move. Pierce them if they rise to the surface. Simmer for 1–1½ hours, until the internal temperature is 160°F (70°C). Lift the sausages from the water and allow to cool. Once cool, refrigerate at once.

Best with...
Carefully peel and slice very thinly. Serve, very cold, with mustard.

Making a chorizo

A combination of smoked paprika and the tanginess produced by the curing process gives chorizo its authentic Spanish flavor. In Spain, wine vinegar is used for curing; in colder climates, 1oz (30g) of starter culture is often used instead. It is vital to follow the instructions for the drying process to the letter.

MAKES 7½–9LB (3.5–4KG) WHEN DRIED

KEEPS FOR UP TO 3 MONTHS IN THE REFRIGERATOR IF WHOLE AND KEPT WRAPPED IN PAPER TOWEL OR A COTTON DISH TOWEL (DON'T SEAL); FOR UP TO 12 MONTHS IN THE FREEZER, WRAPPED TIGHTLY

SPECIAL EQUIPMENT GRINDER; SAUSAGE FILLER; THERMOMETER; HUMIDITY MONITOR; FOOD GRADE PLASTIC GLOVES

COOK 2–3 WEEKS CURING

INGREDIENTS

5 tbsp smoked sweet (mild) paprika

1 tbsp cayenne or hot paprika

4 tbsp finely chopped fresh oregano, or 1 tbsp dried oregano

5½oz (150g) quick dry-curing salt

8lb (3.6kg) lean pork, chilled

1lb 2oz (500g) pork belly, chilled

9fl oz (250ml) white wine vinegar

7–8 large garlic cloves, crushed

10oz (300g) pork back fat, chopped and chilled

20 feet (6 meters) 1½in (35–40mm) natural casings, soaked and one end knotted

SAUSAGE-MAKING TIP

Put the pork belly through the grinder along with the lean meat, to keep it cool and avoid clogging the grinder blades.

1 Mix together the spices, herbs, and curing salt. Grind all the meats through a coarse grinding plate. Sprinkle the vinegar, salt mixture, and garlic over the meat, and mix everything thoroughly.

2 Add the back fat to the mixture, and make sure it is evenly distributed. Grind once again through a fine plate to make filling the skins easier. If the mixture is at all warm, chill it again.

3 Fit the end of a skin over the filler nozzle and pull on the rest. Fill the skins tightly, as they will shrink later. Form into lengths or links, or into rings (see pages 204–205).

4 Tie with string, making a loop. Hang, not touching, for 24–36 hours, at 60–75°F (15–20°C); the warmth causes fermentation, killing bacteria. An airing cupboard is ideal.

5 Dry the chorizos for 2–3 weeks in a cool place at 50–55°F (10–13°C) and 80 percent humidity. A basement or cool, unused garage is suitable. Cover with muslin and leave 2¾–4in (7–10cm) between each sausage. There must be air flow to dry the meat, but also enough humidity to prevent a crust forming that stops the inside from drying out. The chorizo will lose 35 percent of its weight. If the atmosphere is too dry, place a bowl of water between the air flow and the chorizo. If mold forms, wipe the surface of the sausage with vinegar. If a white powdery coating forms, this is ideal.

Best with...
Cook in a paella, or a Spanish bean stew or seafood stew, or jambalaya, or slice onto a homemade pizza.

213

Making a blood sausage

These French-style blood sausages are soft and creamy. The onions may be replaced with cooked vegetables, meat, or grains (rice, barley, or oats), and the spices could be varied to taste. If fresh blood is difficult to source, pure dried pig's blood is sold by butchers' suppliers. Reconstitute according to their directions.

MAKES 15¼–18LB (7–8KG)

KEEPS FOR UP TO 1 WEEK IN THE REFRIGERATOR, WRAPPED; FOR UP TO 4 MONTHS IN THE FREEZER, WRAPPED TIGHTLY IN PLASTIC WRAP

SPECIAL EQUIPMENT
LARGE 4–5 QUART UNBREAKABLE MIXING BOWL; PLASTIC FUNNEL WITH WIDE NECK; LARGE BOILING PAN; FOOD GRADE PLASTIC GLOVES

COOK 20–25 MINUTES

INGREDIENTS

3lb 3oz (1.5kg) pork suet, or pork back fat

2½ cups heavy cream

10½ cups fresh or reconstituted pig's blood

1 tsp quatre-épices (mix of ground pepper, nutmeg, ginger, and cloves)

heaping ¼ cup chopped parsley or sage

1 tsp brown sugar

3oz (85g) salt

6oz (175g) bread crumbs

3lb 3oz (1.5kg) onions, chopped

½ cup unsalted butter, or ½ cup vegetable oil

23 feet (7 meters) ox runners, soaked and one end knotted

SAUSAGE-MAKING TIP
If no skins are available, place the mixture into an oiled dish. Place this in a tray of water and bake at 300°F (150°C) for 30–40 minutes, or until a skewer emerges clean. Slice when cold.

1 Dice the fat into ¼–½in (7–10mm) cubes. Stir the cream into the blood, then mix the spices, herbs, sugar, salt, and bread crumbs together and stir these in, too, making sure everything is evenly mixed.

2 Cook the onions gently in the butter or oil in a large frying pan until softened but not browned. Cool and then add to the blood mixture. Stir in the cubed fat, and mix everything together thoroughly.

3 Knot one end of an ox runner. Fit the open end on to the funnel's nozzle, and pull the remaining skin on to the nozzle. Pour the blood into the funnel.

4 Fill the skin, gripping the nozzle tightly to prevent the skin from slipping off. Fill the skins quite loosely, as the mixture swells when cooked. Knot the end of the skin firmly.

5 Leave the sausage as a coil, or tie it into rings. Divide into lengths, tie the ends with string, fold the skin over the knot and tie again, then tie both ends together. For an alternative, or for tying into links, see page 205.

6 Half-fill the boiling pan with water and place a rack on the bottom. Boil, then remove the pan from the heat. Lower the sausages in carefully, and return to a very low heat. Do not boil, or the sausages may burst.

7 If the sausages float, pierce them with a toothpick. Cook gently for 15 minutes, then pierce them again. If the liquid that emerges is bloody, cook for 5 more minutes, or until the liquid is brown.

8 Drain off the water carefully (the hot sausages are fragile) or lift them out using the rack. Fill a sink with cold water, and cool the sausages in it for 15 minutes before handling. Refrigerate, or cut into slices to cook.

Best with...
Fry slices in butter and serve with sautéed apples.

Glossary

Air dried
Also known as *wind dried,* these sausages are slowly dried in a cool, dry atmosphere.

AOC (Appellation d'Origine Contrôlée)
A French term meaning "controlled designation of origin." Used for food as well as wine.

Artificial casing
See *synthetic casing.*

Banger
A slang term for a sausage, used in most English-speaking countries. The word originated from poor-quality, watery sausages that exploded when cooked.

Back fat
Hard fat from the back of a pig. It is generally diced and used to give flavor and texture.

Binder
Also known as *filler,* this is usually some form of starch used to bind fatty meat or to reduce the meat content.

Black pudding
A type of blood sausage, this is a plump, cooked sausage made of blood and fat, sometimes also containing cereals or vegetables.

Blood sausage
A sausage whose principal ingredient is blood mixed with fat or cereal.

Bratwurst
A smooth sausage of German origin made from raw pounded meat. It is usually grilled.

Brawn
See *head cheese.*

Brühwurst
A category of German smooth sausages that are cooked to 160°F (72°C). They can be eaten cold or cooked again.

Butifarra
A style of sausage from Catalonia, Spain, which does not contain paprika as chorizo does.

Caecum
A pouch at the beginning of the large intestine used as a large sausage casing.

Casing
See *skin.*

Caul fat
A thin, lacy membrane of fat that surrounds the intestines; used to wrap sausage.

Chorizo
A sausage of Spanish origin that is either cured or fresh and contains paprika.

Chouriço
The Portuguese spelling for *chorizo,* also used in former Portuguese colonies.

Cold smoked
A smoking method that uses no heat so that the sausage is flavored but remains uncooked before drying.

Collagen casing
An edible but artificial sausage skin made from collagen: a product derived from animal hides.

Cured sausage
Also known as *fermented sausage,* this is made from fermented sausage, achieved by mixing wine vinegar or curing salt with the meat.

Curing salt
Preservative made from sodium chloride with small amounts of sodium nitrate or sodium nitrite.

DOP
See *PDO.*

Dried sausage
A raw, cured, or cooked sausage that is dried afterwards to preserve it. Refrigeration is not needed.

Fermented sausage
See *cured sausage.*

Filler
See *binder.*

Head cheese
A cooked sausage made from head meat, skin, ears, and tongue, bound together with jelly.

Hot smoked
A method of smoking in which the temperature is increased so that the sausage is cooked as well as flavored.

IGP
See *PGI.*

Kielbasa
The Polish generic word for a sausage. Also means a Polish-style sausage in other countries.

Kochwurst
A category of German sausages that are made from precooked meats that are cooked again. They are usually eaten raw, but some are cooked before being eaten.

Kolbász
The Hungarian generic word for a sausage.

Korv
The Swedish generic word for a sausage.

La chang
The Chinese generic word for a sausage, usually wind dried. There are many alternative spellings.

Lap cheong
See *La chang*. Also spelled Lap Cheung.

Liver sausage
A soft, spreadable cooked sausage that is like a smooth liver pâté encased in a skin. The skin is usually synthetic and inedible.

Loukaniko
The Greek generic word for a sausage.

Lukanka
The Bulgarian generic word for a sausage.

Makkara
The Finnish generic word for a sausage. See also *vursti*.

Merguez
Also spelled *mirqāz* or *mirkās*, a spicy red sausage of North African origin.

Mirqāz/mirkās
See *merguez*.

Natural casing
A sausage skin made from pork, beef, or sheep intestine, caecum, stomach, bladder, or other animal organ.

PDO (Protected Designation of Origin)
Also written DOP. A European Union certification used to protect regional specialities. To qualify, a product must be made traditionally, and every part of the production must take place within the specific region.

PGI (Protected Geographical Indication)
Also written IGP. A European Union certification used to protect regional specialities. To qualify, a product must be made traditionally, and be partially manufactured within the specific region.

Pølse
The Danish and Norwegian generic word for a sausage.

Pudding
A cooked sausage made in a wide casing or stomach. The ingredients may be precooked or raw. They are usually re-cooked before being eaten.

Rohwurst
A category of German fermented or cured sausages. They can be soft or dried, and are often smoked.

Salame
The singular of *salami* (see below). Outside Italy, *salami* is used for both singular and plural.

Salami
A sausage of Italian origin, which can be made of any kind of meat. Salami crudo is a raw, slowly dried sausage. Salami cotto is cooked sausage.

Saucisse
A French generic word for a sausage that is usually, but not invariably, cooked before eating.

Saucisson
A French generic term for a sausage that is usually, but not invariably, sliced and eaten cold.

Sausage filler
A funnel with a plunger used to fill sausage skins, or a machine that forces the sausage into the skins.

Sausage stuffer
See *sausage filler*.

Scalded sausage
A boiled or simmered sausage that is usually boiled again or grilled before eating.

Skin
Also known as a *casing*, this is what contains the sausage. Skins are made from natural, collagen, or synthetic materials.

Soudjouk
Also spelled *sujuk*, *sukuk*, or *sucuk*, a dark red sausage found in the Balkans, Eastern Mediterranean, and North Africa.

Spreadable sausage
A cooked or cured sausage that is soft enough to be spread on bread or toast.

Sujuk/sukuk/sucuk
See *soudjouk*.

Synthetic casing
Also known as *artificial casing*. A sausage skin made from plastic, or sometimes a fibrous material, which is inedible.

TSG (Traditional Speciality Guaranteed)
A European Union certification used to protect traditional specialities. To qualify, a product must be made in the traditional way, but its manufacture is not restricted to a specific area.

Twice-Baked Biscuit
A wheat-based product used to absorb liquid and fat, and which reduces the meat content.

Vursti
A Finnish word for sausage, although *makkara* is more usual.

White sausage
A cooked sausage made from veal, rabbit or poultry, or occasionally just cereal and fat. Also called *white pudding*.

Wind dried
See *air dried*.

Index

Index entries in *italic* are recipes. Where a recipe suggests alternative sausages, it is also indexed under those alternatives, indicated by (*).

INDEX

Thanks

Dorling Kindersley would like to thank the following suppliers who kindly helped us with sourcing the sausages featured in this book.

GERMAN SAUSAGES
Pfälzer Residenz Weinstube
Residenzstr. 1
80085 München, Germany

AUSTRIAN SAUSAGES
Räucherkistl aus Österreich
Viktualienmarkt 3
80331 München, Germany

SWISS SAUSAGES
Boucherie du Simplon
www.boucheriedusimplon.ch
Rue du Simplon 17
1006 Lausanne, Switzerland

Meinen AG
www.cest-si-bon.ch
+41 (0) 3138 94111

Metzgerei Wälchli
Friedhofgasse 9
4500 Solothurn, Switzerland

FRENCH SAUSAGES
La Grande Epicerie de Paris
www.lagrandeepicerie.fr
38 Rue de Sèvres
75007 Paris, France

Une Normande à Londres
www.unenormandealondres.co.uk
Borough Market
Borough High Street
London, SE1 1TL, UK

ITALIAN SAUSAGES
Cibosano
www.cibosano.co.uk
+44 (0) 20 0207 5020

Fiorucci (UK) Ltd.
www.fiorucci.co.uk
+39 (0) 06911931

Gastronomica
www.gastronomica.co.uk
Borough Market
Borough High Street
London, SE1 1TL, UK

I Camisa & Son
61 Old Compton Street
Soho, London, W1D 6HJ, UK

Lina Stores
www.linastores.co.uk
18 Brewer Street
Soho, London, W1F 0SH, UK

Villanova Food Ltd.
www.villanovafood.com
Borough Market
Borough High Street
London, SE1 1TL, UK

SPANISH SAUSAGES
Brindisa
www.brindisa.com
Borough Market
Borough High Street
London, SE1 9AH, UK

Orce Serrano Hams
www.orceserranohams.com
Calle Angel, 15
18858 Orce
Granada, Spain

PORTUGUESE SAUSAGES
Delicias de Portugal
43 Warwick Way
Pimlico, London, SW1V 1QS, UK

BRITISH AND IRISH SAUSAGES
Higginsons of Grange
www.higginsonsofgrange.co.uk
Keswick House
Main Street
Grange Over Sands
Cumbria, LA11 6AB, UK

M. Feller, Son & Daughter
www.mfeller.co.uk
Organic Butcher
54–55 The Oxford Covered Market
Oxford, OX1 3DY, UK

Macken Brothers
www.mackenbros.co.uk
44 Turnham Green Terrace
Chiswick, London, W4 1QP, UK

Musks
www.musks.com
+44 (0) 1638 662626

BELGIAN SAUSAGES
Beenhouwerij Declerck-Cloetens
www.dcquality.com
Veeweydestraat 4
1070 Anderlecht, Belgium

DANISH SAUSAGES
Danish Food Direct
www.danishfooddirect.co.uk
+44 (0) 1234 888788

SWEDISH SAUSAGES
Koberg Vilt
www.kobergvilt.se
Koberg 10
466 91 Sollebrunn, Sweden

EASTERN EUROPEAN SAUSAGES
Patson Delicatessen
www.patsonlocal.co.uk
87/89 Whetley Lane
Bradford, BD8 9DS, UK

NORTH AND SOUTH AMERICAN SAUSAGES
Bell's Meat and Poultry
www.jackbellsmeats.com
401 North Fraley Street
Kane, PA 16735, USA

Esposito's Finest Quality Sausage Products
www.espositosausage.com
354 West 38th Street
New York, NY 10018, USA

Hartmann's Old World Sausage
www.hartmannssausage.com
2640 Brickyard Road
Canandaigua, NY 14424, USA

Mello's Chourico
www.melloschourico.com
63 North Court Street
Fall River, MA 02720, USA

Ottomanelli & Sons Prime Meat Market
285 Bleecker Street
New York, NY 10014, USA

Salumeria Biellese
www.salumeriabiellese.com
378 8th Avenue
New York, NY 10001, USA

**Special America's BBQ Inc./
Mr. Tango Sausages**
www.mrtangocorp.com
Miami, FL 33296, USA

SAUSAGE MAKING EQUIPMENT
Kenwood UK
www.kenwoodworld.com/uk
+44 (0) 2392 476000

Weschenfelder Sausage Making Supplies
www.weschenfelder.co.uk
+44 (0) 1642 247524

Authors

Nichola Fletcher has been a writer, consultant, and speaker on all things meat-related for more than 30 years. Having pioneered the first venison farm in the UK with her husband John in 1973, she has since authored seven titles, including the Gourmand World Cookbook Award-winning *Ultimate Venison Cookery* (2007), and contributed to major publications such as *The Financial Times* and *Gastronomica*. She also wrote the meat chapters in DK's *The Illustrated Cook's Book of Ingredients* (2010). Running her own farm means that Nichola has hands-on knowledge of producing award-winning meat, and she shares her passion and expertise by running workshops and tutored game tastings. She lives in Scotland.

Caroline Bretherton has worked in the food industry for more than 15 years. As well as running her own catering company, Manna Food, and eatery, the Manna Café, Caroline works in television and print media. She has authored *The Kitchen Garden Cookbook* (2011) and *Illustrated Step-by-step Baking* (2011), both published by Dorling Kindersley.

Acknowledgments

Nichola Fletcher would like to thank:
Paul Broda, John Clifford, Adi Dänzer, Ralf Lautenschläger, Susan Lendrum (Germany, Austria, and Switzerland); Francine Lossois, Sue Style (France); Antoinetta Kelly of the Italian Trade Commission, Mark Millon (Italy); Maria José Sevilla (Spain); Ricardo Chorão, Stella Fletcher, João Guedes, Restaurant QB, Filipe Pedro & Joana, Restaurant Pedro Lemos, Joana Ribeiro, Teresa Tavares (Portugal); Peter Gott, Claire Macleod, Robert Weschenfelder (UK and Ireland); Sophie Bouallegue (The Low Countries); Rasmus Lomborg, Annica and Ing-Marie Sandstrom, Johan Trygve Solheim (Scandinavia); Karolina Jankowicz, Robert Szaniawski of the Polish Embassy, Tomasz Zalewski (Poland); Ludek Bartos, Jitka Bartosova, Tatyana Jakovskaya, Petr Janovsky, Kaspars Jansons (Central and Eastern Europe and Russia); Alexandros Konstantinou (Eastern Mediterranean); Kevin Belton, Alison Fletcher, Bud Graske, Mari Harpur (USA and Canada); Vanessa and Gabriel Hernandez (Central and South America); Fuchsia Dunlop, Deh-ta Hsuing, Will Yorke (Asia); Andrew Easdale (Australia & New Zealand).

Dorling Kindersley would like to thank:
Ralf Lautenschläger (Germany, Austria, and Switzerland consultant); Kate Curnes (US consultant); Andrew Roff for invaluable help in making the sausage shoots possible; Jane Lawrie for food styling; Luis Peral and Kathryn Wilding for art direction; Jane Bamforth, Jan Fullwood, Laura Fyfe, Katy Greenwood, and Natalie Seldon for recipe testing; Sue Morony and Aditi Batra for proofreading; Marie Lorimer for indexing; Rebecca Warren and Allison Singer for organizing the US shoot; Will Yorke for organizing the China shoot; Navidita Thapa, Neha Ahuja, and Charis Bhagianathan for organizing the India shoot; Rosie Adams for organizing the Australia shoot.

Special thanks go to everyone who helped us to source the sausages: Carlos Declerck at Beenhouwerij Declerck-Cloetens; Boucherie du Simplon; Totuccio Castiglione at Cibosano; Vivian at Danish Food Direct; Mitzi Feller at M. Feller, Son & Daughter; Vicki Davis at Fiorucci; Mark at Higginsons of Grange; Maria Silfverschiöld at Koberg Vilt; Max and Max at Lina Stores; Meinen AG; Metzgerei Wälchli; Chris Sheen at Musks; Iain and Gayle at Orce Serrano Hams; Dennis at Patson Ltd; Johannes Müller at Pfälzer Residenz Weinstube; Martin Babler at Räucherkistl—Spezialitäten aus Österreich; Rosie Cowen at Villanova Food; Tracie Jefferson at Weschenfelder and Sons Ltd; Jerome Tabarie at Une Normande à Londres; Elke Homburg and Kristine Harth of DK Verlag; Rachel Watson, Caroline Lauder, Vanessa Cerchia, and Louise Buckens of DK IPL; Sonia Charbonnier; Silke Spingies; Stella Fletcher; Charlotte Seymour; Layla Theiner; Sue Style; Jitka Bartosova and Petr Janovsky; and Daniel Stewart, Agata Jakubowska, and Artur Cysiuk of Pearson Catering Department for helping us store 322 sausages.